The
Weekend Mechanic's
Guide to

CAR CARE
& REPAIR

by Joseph L. Koenig

A Dell Book

A Dell Book

Published by Dell Publishing Co., Inc.
1 Dag Hammarskjold Plaza
New York, New York 10017

Copyright © 1979 by Dell Publishing Co., Inc.

ISBN: 0-440-69581-3

CONTENTS

Introduction

Intimidating, isn't it? All shiny steel and glass, one of your most expensive purchases, an inscrutable labyrinth of mechanical devices whose workings are beyond mortal comprehension. And it's broken. At least it's not running the way it's supposed to. There's a funny noise under the hood that won't go away and those vibrations are driving you crazy. What to do? What to do?

The first thing every motorist should know about car trouble is that unless it's serious—which is not very often—he or she probably can fix it without professional help. True, unless you're mechanically inclined and already a confirmed do-it-yourselfer, that doesn't sound especially like fun. But consider the alternatives: The inconvenience of bringing the car to and from a repair shop and skyrocketing repair bills which can take all the fun out of driving. Does that sound any better?

Sure you're afraid to pick up a screwdriver and wrench and dig into the guts of your car. It's a messy job and you're convinced you'll foul things up so badly that a mechanic will be needed just to undo the damage. Objection over-ruled! If you don't go poking around where you don't belong, such as the transmission or suspension system, the worst that can happen is that you'll have to call a mechanic, which is what you'd planned in the first place.

Besides, why shouldn't you learn to make basic repairs on your own car? Because you drive it, you know it better than anyone else and that makes you the person best qualified to tend to its needs.

And there are other reasons, too, for learning to fix your car. It's dangerous not to at least be able to recognize the symptoms of trouble which may lead to expensive repair bills, or, worse, an accident. Recent surveys indicate that motorists who are ignorant of how their car works have as many as 50 percent more accidents than drivers who know what makes their cars go.

Thumb through this book to see what first aid for your car entails. You'll find that one of the essentials is a small collection of basic tools—screwdrivers, pliers, adjustable wrenches, etc. View these purchases as long-term investments, so buy the best. And, before we start, there's one more thing. Have fun as you work and learn.

We'll begin with something easy, a preventive maintenance procedure, which, if attended to regularly, will save you lots of grief on the highway.

CHECKING YOUR CAR'S EXHAUST SYSTEM

Since one of the chief byproducts of gasoline combustion is carbon dioxide, an odorless, colorless, poisonous gas which generally is discharged through the tailpipes, a comprehensive check of your car's exhaust system is a must at least twice a year. Most faulty exhaust systems do not make a telltale sound to alert you to trouble. Yet, every time you drive your car, harmful acids that eat away the inside of the exhaust system are produced. In most cars two to three years old, the deterioration caused by those acids already is in an advanced state. The only way it can be detected is visually.

It will be easier to examine the exhaust system if your car is raised. If a lift or a pair of ramps is not available, do *not* jack up the car. Instead, use a creeper (a low, padded dolly that allows you to lie on your back and slide under a car). Exhaust systems heat up quickly, so be sure to keep your face and other exposed areas away from metal parts. Also be sure to wear safety glasses or goggles at all times to keep bits of rust out of your eyes.

Because it is subject to failure more quickly than other parts of the exhaust system, begin your examination with the muffler (see illustration at chapter's end). That is the oval container, about two feet long, mounted toward the rear of the underbody. Its purpose is to choke off the exhaust roar of the engine and it accomplishes that task by shunting the exhaust through a series of baffle plates and perforated tubes to break up sound.

A muffler usually begins failing from the inside out as the harmful acids accumulate and eat away at the metal. It also is susceptible to external damage from water, road salt, rocks and high curbs. Use a flashlight to make a visual inspection of the muffler, paying particular attention to any holes and split seams. When the engine is off and the muffler is cool, run your hand along the metal. If you collect a large amount of rust particles, it may not mean that the muffler is about to disintegrate, but it is a good indication that the time to replace it is soon.

Another way to test for potential trouble is to tap the muffler with a metal tool. A healthy muffler should emit a clear, ringing sound, while a dull thud probably means the muffler is about to go. If you succeed in banging the tool through the muffler, don't berate yourself. The inside of the muffler was so eaten away by acid that it was about to disintegrate anyway.

After inspecting the muffler, it is time for a look at the exhaust pipe which runs the length of the car from the muffler to the exhaust manifold on the cylinder head. Again, use a metal tool to tap the steel pipe from one end to the other, checking for signs of wear. Be especially alert for rust, cracks, holes and any dents which look as though they might impede the flow of exhaust fumes inside the pipe. Damaged pipes should be replaced at once to prevent back pressure in the exhaust system which leads to poor engine performance.

A common trouble spot is the connection between the exhaust pipe and exhaust manifold. White powdery deposits around this connection means that the gasket which seals the joint is rotten or that the bolts which secure the exhaust pipe to the manifold have come loose. In either event, the white powder is a sure sign that exhaust fumes are leaking out of the system.

Try to tighten the bolts with a wrench. If they appear to be tight already the problem is with the gasket. You can replace it yourself by disconnecting the exhaust pipe from the exhaust manifold, cleaning both surfaces thoroughly and inserting a new gasket. Tighten the bolts as much as possible.

Now turn on the engine and listen carefully for hissing or rumbling sounds, which also indicate a leak. Make a visual check for smoke leaks, paying special attention to the exhaust pipe, resonators (secondary mufflers located at the rear of the exhaust system on many cars), the connector pipe and the tail pipe. If you find that fumes are seeping through a faulty clamp, remove the clamp and spread a sealing compound around the joint before replacing it. If the leak is coming from a component of the exhaust system, have a mechanic replace it.

The inspection isn't over until you have checked the hangers, which are the rubber and fabric loops which secure the exhaust system to the car. When the engine is cold, grab the system with your hands and give it a good shake. Excessive movement probably means that a hanger should be replaced, as do any signs of cracking or fraying.

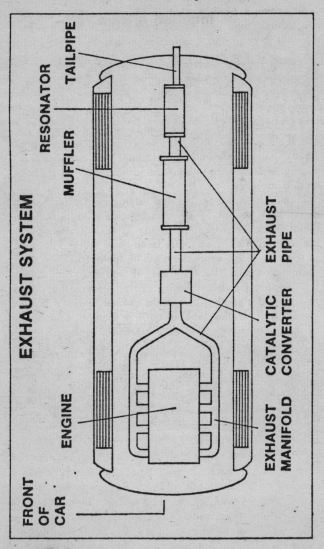

EXHAUST SYSTEM

FRONT OF CAR

ENGINE

MUFFLER

RESONATOR

TAILPIPE

EXHAUST PIPE

CATALYTIC CONVERTER

EXHAUST MANIFOLD

Inflation Is Here

Although the current trend is toward bulkier tires, there is no reason for even the puniest of motorists to have much trouble changing a flat if he follows one simple bit of philosophy: Let the equipment take care of the hard work. Save your back and arms for the important business of driving, sitting up straight and gripping the steering wheel.

Because no one has much confidence in the jacks which auto manufacturers supply with their cars, it is comforting to perform as many tire-changing procedures as possible while all four wheels still are on the ground. A healthy fear of the standard tire jack is nothing to be ashamed of. Perhaps it even should be cultivated. In most cases, the jack is too spindly to support your car adequately and is susceptible to slippage, either in the mechanism or at the base. Even worse, should you be lucky enough to raise your wheel high enough to change the tire you have probably achieved a tenuous balance at best; lower the car as soon as possible.

To speed you along your way, use the pointed end of the tire iron to pry the hubcap from the afflicted wheel. Don't fling the cap away like a frisbee, but keep it close at hand to prevent neighborhood youngsters from running off with it and also to use as a receptacle for the lug nuts. These nuts—most wheels contain five—should be loosened with the wrench-like end of the tire iron while the car still is on the ground.

You are now ready to jack up the wheel, but, first, use the wooden chocks in your trunk—or handy bricks or rocks—to block the end of the car opposite from the flat and prevent any chance of rolling. Then place the jack where your owner's manual advises—usually the bumper, or somewhere on the frame. If you have a crank-type jack, insert the shaft in the base and the handle in the sliding gear and begin pumping away. If your car is equipped with the more compact screw-type jack you must use the tire iron to twist the screw until the car is raised.

Don't jack up the car any higher than is absolutely necessary. If the flat is a dime's thickness above the ground, you should have enough working room.

When the car is high enough, remove the jack handle to prevent accidents and twist off the loosened lug nuts by hand. When all five are cached in the hubcap, grab the tire at the 9 and 3 o'clock positions and wiggle it gently toward you. Don't yank hard at it or you might end up with it in your lap. Once the tire is off the wheel, continue wiggling it past the fender. Then rest it against the side of the car; it is heavy to retrieve from the ground.

With the damaged tire out of the way, open the trunk and unscrew the wing nut which holds the spare in place. Try to roll the spare down onto the ground, which is much easier on the back muscles than dragging it out of the trunk on its side. Don't let the tire get away from you. As soon as you get the tire rolling out of the trunk, take a couple of steps backward and cradle it in your hands as it hits the ground. Then roll it toward the bare wheel.

Now comes the hardest part of the entire procedure— lifting the tire back onto the wheel. If the car was not jacked up too high, that should not be beyond almost anyone's physical capabilities. If the holes on the spare are too high or low to fit on the wheel, rest the spare against the wheel with the holes as close as you can get them to the studs. Then jack the car up or down until you can slide the tire onto the wheel.

Now replace all the lug nuts, twisting them by hand as tight as you can get them. Lower the tire to the ground and finish tightening the nuts with the tire iron. Place the hub cap into position against the wheel and hammer it into place with the side of your fist or rubber mallet if you have one.

All that remains to be done, prior to getting back on the road, is to get the flat tire out of the way. Because it is best to have it repaired at the next gas station you come to, don't bother about returning it to the trunk. Roll it into the rear seat well, if possible, and forget about it. The service station attendant will put it in the trunk for you after repairing it.

It is arguable that the price of new tires is rising even faster than the price of new cars. To maximize their life, it is a good idea to rotate tires every 6000 miles. Since the whole purpose of this procedure is to save money, you might as well do the job yourself.

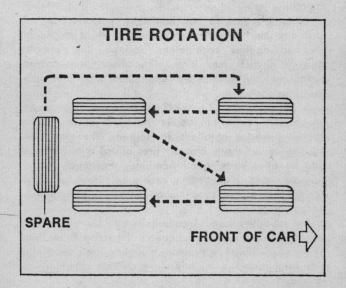

TIRE ROTATION

SPARE

FRONT OF CAR ⇨

Begin by loosening the nuts on all four wheels. Then jack up the left front wheel and replace it with the spare. Next, remove the left rear tire and replace it with the tire just taken from the left front. Then replace the right front tire with the former left rear and the right rear with the former right front. The job is done when you have placed the remaining tire in the trunk. (See illustration preceding page.)

If repeated faithfully every 6000 miles or so, this procedure will increase tire life by evening out tread wear. However, there is one word of caution which must not be ignored: *If your car is equipped with radial tires, normal tire rotation must be avoided.* Unlike common bias ply tires, radial tires contain cords which run vertically between the beads and parallel to the movement of the car. Belted tires should only be rotated from front to rear and from rear to front on the same side of the car.

When it's time to buy new tires, performance and cost are the two main considerations which should be weighed against each other. Today's tires can be roughly divided into three distinctive types—conventional bias-ply, bias-belted and radial ply. (See illustration opposite.)

In the conventional bias-ply, two or more nylon, rayon or polyester cords run across the width of the tire at opposing angles of about 35 degrees. The most inexpensive of the three, bias-ply tires afford a comfortable ride at all speeds, good handling, reasonably strong sidewalls and high rolling resistance. However, bias-ply tires wear out sooner than either of their higher-priced competitors.

The middle-priced, bias-belted tire has a two-ply belt of fiberglass or steel beneath the tread in addition to the corded plies. It provides a slightly less comfortable ride than bias-plys, slightly more difficult handling, but lasts much longer.

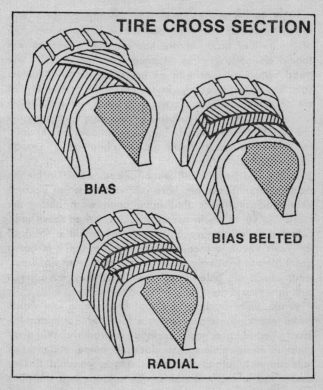

TIRE CROSS SECTION

BIAS

BIAS BELTED

RADIAL

The most expensive of the three is the radial tire. Its cord plies run vertically between the beads (the casings of steel wire which help hold the tire onto the wheel rim). The plies are augmented by belts of steel, fiberglass, or man-made fiber under the tread. Except at high speeds, radial tires provide a rather rough ride. But they grip the road better than any other tire, have a high resistance to lateral movement and scuffing and last much longer than the other types of tires.

Even the most pampered tires eventually grow old. When the tread has gone down to a thickness of 1/16 of an inch or less, the tire has become a hazard and should be gotten rid of at once. You can measure the tread with a ruler or with an otherwise almost valueless coin known as a penny. Insert the edge of the top of the coin into the tire groove. If it does not sink below the top of Lincoln's head, the treads are worn and the tire should be discarded. The penny should be retained for further use as a tread gauge, about all it is good for these days.

Some tires have tread wear indicators built in by the manufacturer. These are hard rubber bars which become visible across treads that have been worn below the crucial 1/16 of an inch safety factor. When these indicators crop up in two or three spots within a third of the tire's circumference, replace the tire. But it is not a good idea to trust your safety to the appearance of tread wear indicators unless you know that they have been built into your tires.

While we're on the subject of tire care, a few words about checking air pressure are in order. To guarantee long mileage, tires must be inflated properly. When air pressure is insufficient, tire sidewalls bulge. As the tire rolls unevenly along the road surface, constant flexing causes the fabric in the sidewalls to crack and the plies to separate. Complete tire failure sometimes follows. (See illustration opposite.) If tires are under-inflated, the outer treads also suffer excessive wear because they must support virtually the entire weight of the car. The center tread, pushed clear of the road by the bulging sidewalls, remains almost unworn.

Over-inflation, while not as dangerous as under-inflation, equally is harmful to tire life. When a tire is over-inflated, it is the center of the tread which receives all the wear. The outer treads, raised clear of the road, show almost no wear at all. Over-inflated tires also do a poor job of absorbing road shocks, producing an uncomfortable ride and placing a great deal of strain on the fabric, which has been known to give too many bumps.

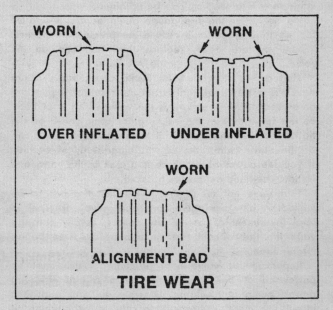

WORN

WORN

OVER INFLATED   **UNDER INFLATED**

WORN

ALIGNMENT BAD

TIRE WEAR

To check the pressure in your tires, it is essential to have a pressure gauge—a cheap, handy stainless steel instrument available at any auto supply store. It also is necessary to know the tire pressure in **psi** (pounds per square inch) that the manufacturer recommends for his product.

Because pressure increases as tires heat up during use, it is best to make your check in the morning, before your car has been driven.

To take a reading, simply unscrew the cap from the

end of the tire valve and place the rounded end of the gauge in the valve. Make sure that the pin in the gauge is pressing against the pin in the valve. The pressure inside the tire will push against the sliding part of the valve so that a reading can be obtained.

Do not press the tire gauge down against the valve for too long or you will reduce the pressure in the tire. When you are done, replace the small cap on the valve.

That cap is not air tight. Quite often, when a tire develops a slow leak that is not the result of a puncture or a break at the bead, it is the valve which is at fault. To test for a leak at the valve, place some saliva on the tip of a finger and transfer it to the air inlet at the end of the valve (when the cap is unscrewed, of course). If you see any bubbles, there is a leak in the valve and it should be fixed as soon as possible.

That does not mean that the entire tire has to be junked. A new tire valve core and valve core tool, a total investment of just a few dollars, usually can salvage the tire without further problem or, even better, further expense.

Replacing the valve is a procedure which must be performed at a service station or anywhere else that an air pump is available. Unscrew the cap and then insert the core remover into the valve, turning it counter-clockwise until it starts to screw out of the valve.

Now, pinching it tightly between fingers, twist the core out of the valve and allow the tire to deflate. When the air pressure is significantly reduced, insert the new core by hand, twisting it as tightly as you can. Finishing tightening it with the valve core tool and then inflate the tire by hand pump or station air hose to the proper pressure.

How to Avoid Assault on Your Battery

Maintaining a clean battery is one of the simplest jobs on your car. But just because it is easy does not mean that it can be ignored. If you've ever had to shell out 20 dollars for a tow to a gas station because you thought your battery was dead, only to be told that there was nothing more the matter than dirty, corroded terminals or cables, you already understand the importance of battery care.

Every battery has positive and negative terminals. If an electrical conductor such as a screwdriver were stretched from one to the other, a short circuit would result with lots of sparks. Surprisingly, dirt, too, is a relatively efficient conductor of electricity. More than one motorist has learned the hard way that it is possible for dirt to slowly drain away a battery's power without any telltale sparks.

A more common reason for needless power loss is corrosion of the battery terminal connections. That corrosion, in the form of white deposits which collect on the terminals as the result of chemical action inside the battery, serves as an unwanted insulator, preventing current from passing from the terminal to the battery cable. Often such corrosion gathers only at the point of contact; outside, the cable-terminal connection appears to be fine.

An ideal, cheap battery terminal cleaner is a solution of baking soda and water that is strong enough to fizz. Before applying it—and whenever performing any job on your car's battery—change into your least favorite clothing. You may be surprised to find how quickly a stray drop of battery acid can eat through the toughest fabrics. It is even more important not to smoke; the hydrogen gas given off by the battery is highly explosive.

To start the cleaning, cover the tiny vent holes in the fluid caps with masking tape, then pour the baking soda solution over the battery. When the foaming stops, scrub the battery with a brush until all traces of dirt and grease are gone and then rinse off all the residue with water.

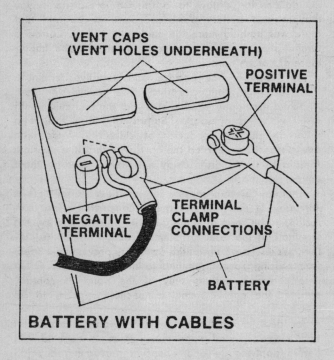

VENT CAPS
(VENT HOLES UNDERNEATH)

POSITIVE TERMINAL

NEGATIVE TERMINAL

TERMINAL CLAMP CONNECTIONS

BATTERY

BATTERY WITH CABLES

Now you are ready to loosen the battery cable clamps. Remove the ground, or negative cable first to prevent sparking (unless your car has a positive ground system, in which case reverse the procedure). Frequently, the corrosive agents which collect on the terminals are so strong that they destroy the nut and bolt and make it impossible to loosen the clamp. Penetrating oil is one solution to that problem. Another is a battery terminal puller, which looks something like a gourmet corkscrew. If the clamp or cable is very corroded, get rid of it and replace them later. Some cars are equipped with spring-type cable clamps and do not have clamp nuts or bolts. They can be removed easily from the battery with blunt-nosed pliers.

After removing both cable clamps, scrub them with steel wool or a wire battery terminal-and-clamp brush. Scrub the terminals, too. Don't stop until everything is bright and shiny, especially the inside of the clamps.

Before replacing the clamps, take a look at the battery hold-down and support case, which are very vulnerable to corrosion. Lift out the battery, being careful not to spill any of the acid, and remove hold-down bolts and brackets. Then scrape away all the dirt and corrosion so that you can apply a coat of rust inhibiting primer and, later, a coat or two of paint or corrosion-resistant grease to the support, the hold-down bolts and the hold-down.

When the battery is locked securely into the support again, replace the clamps on the terminals and tighten them. Be careful not to cross the cables.

That cold winter morning every motorist dreads has just dawned gray and icy. You left your lights on last night and now your battery is too weak to start your car. Even worse, you don't have the jumper cables you promised yourself you'd buy. It's a good thing for you that your neighbor or the guy in the next parking space has a set of cables and time to spare to give you a boost. But where to begin?

First of all, make certain that your friend's battery is the same size as yours. It doesn't matter if your car has an alternator and his has a generator, or vice-versa, or even if your car is positive ground and his is negative ground. Just make sure you attach the cables properly. (See illustration opposite.)

Have your benefactor drive his car close to yours, so that you will not have any difficulty in getting the cables to reach from one battery to the other. Then raise the hood on both cars. Because batteries produce hydrogen gas, which is highly explosive, and we are going to produce a spark, which might possibly trigger it, raise the fluid caps on both batteries. After flapping open the caps, locate the positive post on each battery. It is the larger of the two posts and should be marked with a plus sign.

Attatch a red alligator clamp to each positive post. The other battery post, the thinner one, is the negative post. Connect both negatives with the cable that has the black alligator clamps. Now take another look and make sure the batteries are linked positive to positive and negative to negative. (The negative clamp to the dead car also may be grounded on its engine block.)

Have your friend get behind the wheel of his car and start up the engine. He should keep his foot moderately heavy on the gas, not letting the engine race, but keeping it above a high idle. It is your turn to start your car now, so just twist the key and touch the gas pedal. *Voila!* Disconnect the cables, shut your hood, thank your friend and go buy jumpers.

After jump-starting your car, the simplest way to recharge the battery is to go for a drive in the country. A distance of 15 to 20 miles at a speed of about 50 miles per hour will suffice. If you haven't the time or the inclination for such a trip, your best bet is to use a battery charger.

If your preference is for the battery charger, there are two options open to you—fast or slow charging.

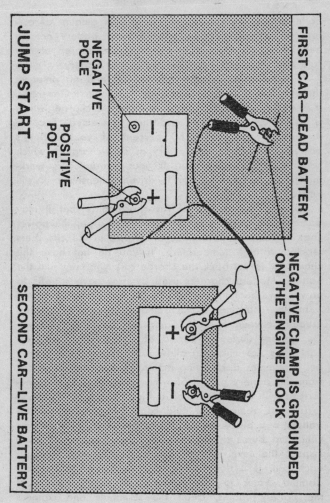

JUMP START

FIRST CAR—DEAD BATTERY

NEGATIVE POLE

POSITIVE POLE

NEGATIVE CLAMP IS GROUNDED ON THE ENGINE BLOCK

SECOND CAR—LIVE BATTERY

Both require the passage of a specific amount of current through the battery. Should your battery not be healthy, it will not accept or retain the charge at any rate and your best bet is to buy a new battery.

A fast charge induces between 50 and 60 amperes through the battery in less than two hours. Generally, it is performed with a portable high-rate charger which is rolled up to the car and then connected. Because it restores only about 80 percent of your battery's power, it is not as satisfactory as slow-charging, which restores 100 percent. But, if your alternator is working properly and the car is driven extensively, it will suffice.

The negative aspect of fast-charging is that it may damage the battery. During a quick charge, the power must be restored before the electrolyte in the chambers reaches a high temperature. If you do not have the know-how to cut back the charge rate you may ruin the battery. Modern chargers used by pros have cut-offs to prevent overheating.

In slow-charging, a much smaller amount of current, usually between 5 and 7 amperes, is passed through the battery during a period of about 12 hours. Not only does slow-charging allow restoration of full power, but it reverses discharging action by removing sulphates from the battery plates. Slow-charging generally is performed with a device called a trickle charger.

To start, remove the fluid caps from the top of the battery and place a rag loosely over the holes to prevent acid burns should the electrolyte bubble up. Now inspect the level of the electrolyte (battery fluid) in each cell. If it does not extend to the fill mark, add distilled water to the proper level. Then disconnect the battery cables, clean the terminals and connect the positive cable of the charger to the positive battery terminal and the negative charger cable to the negative terminal. Plug the charger into a 110-volt power source.

Turn on the charger, adjusting it to between 5 and 15 amperes. No automatic device can be expected to work properly always, so, even if your charger has an automatic shut-off, you should use a hydrometer to check each cell every hour to make sure the battery is not over-charging. Better yet, use a hydrometer with a built-in thermometer and make certain the temperature never rises above 125 degrees. Otherwise, touch the battery case with your hand from time to time to be sure it is not getting too hot.

When the electrolyte begins bubbling actively, lower the rate of charge. Remember that the battery is fully charged when the specific gravity reading in each cell, as measured by the hydrometer, is 1.260.

You should perform a hydrometer test on your battery once each season to make sure that it is still at full strength. Put simply, a hydrometer is a device that measures the specific gravity of battery fluid in comparison to that of water. Battery acid weighs more than water and so the heavier the fluid, the more fully charged the battery.

Prior to performing the hydrometer test, make a visual check of your battery. Examine the casing for cracks and bulges, look for corrosion at the terminals and fraying in the cables. Then look inside.

Flip open the fluid caps and inspect the electrolyte in each cell. If the battery appears to be low on fluid, fill a rubber syringe with distilled water and add to each cell just enough to bring the fluid level up to the indicator mark. Make certain the fluid does not go above the mark. Before any hydrometer test, allow your car to run for at least a quarter of an hour, so that the distilled water will mix with the electrolyte. Let the car cool for about half an hour.

When the time has passed, place the end of the hydrometer in one of the cells and squeeze the rubber bulb until you have drawn enough fluid to float the indicator inside the tube. Now take a reading. A specific gravity of 1.260 to 1.300 indicates the battery is fully charged. A reading of 1.230 to 1.250 in each cell shows that the battery is somewhat low on charge, but probably will perform satisfactorily. Any reading below 1.250 indicates time to buy a new battery.

In recent years, "maintenance-free" batteries, which retain all their fluid, have, become popular. Other batteries normally lose about two ounces of fluid every 1000 miles on the road. If your battery's exceeding that, check car's charging system.

A loose fan belt is a common cause of charging system failure. To check it, press with your fingers halfway between the alternator and fan. If it gives more than half an inch, tighten it. If it is cracked or frayed, or if the inside is glazed and shiny, replace it.

To tighten or replace a fan belt, loosen the alternator mounting bolt on the bottom of the alternator and the adjusting bolt on top with a wrench. Push alternator toward engine block by taking the belt between your fingers and snapping it sharply upward. In cars equipped with air conditioning or power steering, smaller belts may need loosening to provide access to fan belt. If fan belt is missing, or torn, use handle of a hammer as a lever to push alternator toward block.

After removing the old belt, slide the replacement into the crankshaft and pulley grooves. Then pull the alternator until the belt is fairly snug. Tighten by pushing the alternator away from the fan with the hammer handle. When there is about half an inch of play in the belt, tighten the adjustment bolt and pivot bolt. After securing the alternator bracket, start engine and run 15 minutes at different speeds. Reinspect tension then and after driving 100 miles.

Starting and Sparking

Battery failure is not the only reason your car may not want to start. The trouble could be with the electric starter, itself. Fortunately, it is relatively rare for this device to malfunction and, before blaming it for any problem, you should check out the battery and the wiring. You might also seek the advice of a mechanic. If, indeed, the verdict is a burned-out starter, it is not the end of the world.

Electric starters are inexpensive, do not require a great deal of skill to work with and are easily accessible under the hood. The starter motor on most cars is bolted to the flywheel housing on the driver's side of the engine. When an electric current is received from the battery, a drive gear on the starter spins. As it meshes with the gear teeth on the flywheel, internal components are set into motion and the engine starts running.

If you are going to replace your car's starter with a minimum of effort, you should be equipped with a jack, a couple of jackstands and a creeper, a padded dolly that allows you to lie on your back and slide under the car.

Now that you've gathered your equipment, raise the hood and disconnect the ground cable from your battery terminal. Then find the starter and get a good idea of where it is located. From now on you will see it only from underneath the engine.

Slide under the car on your creeper and remove all wires connected to the starter, labeling them with masking tape tags so that you'll be able to replace them properly later on. Then loosen the mounting bolts on the starter, but do not remove them right away. First, prepare yourself for the some 15-pound weight of the starter. (See illustration next page.)

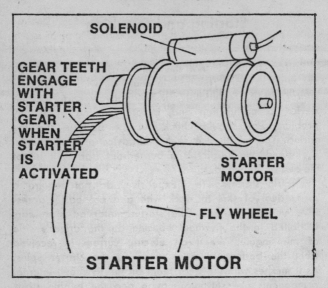

SOLENOID

GEAR TEETH
ENGAGE
WITH
STARTER
GEAR
WHEN
STARTER
IS
ACTIVATED

STARTER
MOTOR

FLY WHEEL

STARTER MOTOR

When you feel secure, take off the bolts and bring the starter toward you. Put it somewhere out of the harm's way and replace it with the new starter, tightening the mounting bolts and reconnecting all the wires according to instruction on your labels. Make certain to use internal tooth or lock washers on all wire connections. Then reconnect the battery ground cable and test the quality of your work by turning on the ignition.

Ignition Systems

Because nearly all American cars of post-1973 vintage come equipped with electronic ignition systems, which do not have points or condensers, and because they also are a hassle to fool around with, we will not bother with the distributor. Be warned that electronic ignition systems are very sophisticated mechanisms and that *only a trained mechanic* should touch them. If yours is an older car with a standard ignition system and you are determined to get inside the distributor, your best bet is to buy a tune-up kit which contains everything you need for the job, including instructions. We'll begin our discussion of your car's ignition system just outside the distributor, at the ignition wires.

Those wires, one for each cylinder to the spark plugs, carry an electric charge from the distributor to the spark plugs. Their average life usually is in the three-year, or 30,000 mile range, but often they do not show their age. Rather than wait until that day when they will not carry their load, replace them before that time. If any of the wires are cracked, frayed, oil-soaked or turning hard and brittle at their connection with the distributor or spark plugs, change them. If you are going to replace one or two wires, you might as well replace all of them. The others can't be in much better shape.

To avoid a lot of unnecessary sizing and cutting, buy an ignition wire set which contains wires that already are cut to your car's specifications. Each wire should have a boot that fits over the spark plug at one end and a nipple that attaches to the distributor cap at the other. (See illustration next page.)

Raise the hood and remove the air filter cover over the carburetor so that you will have easy access to all the wires. Grab the rubber boot on the spark plug *farthest* from the distributor and twist it off. Then trace the wire back to the distributor cap and snap it out. Don't throw the old wire away. Use it to compare against the wires in the ignition wire set until you find one that is the same size. Snap the nipple of this new wire into the distributor and push the boot over the spark plug from which the old wire has been removed. Push down hard on each end to insure a good connection. Do the same with all the other wires in the set you purchased until you have re-wired all the spark plugs.

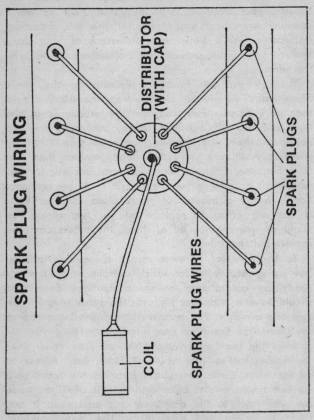

DISTRIBUTOR (WITH CAP)

SPARK PLUG WIRING

SPARK PLUGS

SPARK PLUG WIRES

COIL

Now locate the high tension wire connecting the center tower of the distributor with the ignition coil tower. Remove it from the ignition coil first and then from the distributor, replacing it with the proper wire from the ignition wire set. Put back the air filter cover, lower the hood and throw the old wires away.

If your ignition wires are sound, but you're still having a hard time starting the car on rainy or snowy days, the problem might be wet wires. If you hear crackling noises under the hood or see sparks at the wires in the vicinity of the distributor cap, you can be all but certain that is the cause.

To deal with this trouble you should keep on hand a commercial moisture dispersing spray. Simply aim the can at the wires near the distributor cap and coat them with fluid. Then spray along the length of the wires to the spark plug book and give them a good dousing, too. Also spray the wire leading from the distributor to the coil. Mop up the excess with a clean rag and then try the car. If it starts, lower the hood and get going. If it doesn't, use some more of the spray.

At the heart of your car's ignition system are the spark plugs, whose job it is to ignite the explosive mixture of air and gasoline which powers the engine. A spark plug is made up of steel and ceramic casing construction around two wires with ends positioned so close that an electric spark from the distributor can jump the gap. As this high-voltage charge passes from one piece of metal to the other, it ignites the mixture in the cylinder and the engine turns.

Because there is no place for spark plugs to hide at the moment of explosion, they experience a very high mortality rate. Under normal conditions, they should be replaced every 12,000 miles.

Never fool around with spark plugs while the engine still is hot. That way you stand a fair chance of burning yourself on the nearby manifold. Make your last trip in the car before letting the engine cool to pick up a set of new plugs, a rachet wrench with spark plug socket and a wire spark plug gauge.

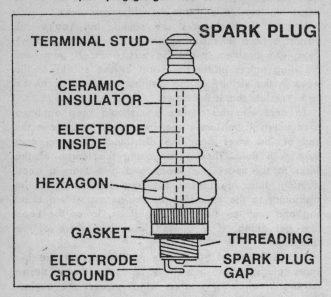

SPARK PLUG

TERMINAL STUD

CERAMIC INSULATOR

ELECTRODE INSIDE

HEXAGON

GASKET

THREADING

ELECTRODE GROUND

SPARK PLUG GAP

When the engine is cooled off, locate the spark plug wires and grasp one by the rubber boot. Twist it gently off the spark plug and then use a rag to wipe away the crud on the surrounding engine block. If you prefer to remove all your spark plugs from the engine before gapping and replacing them, it is all right to do so. Label the wires with adhesive tape so that you do not mix the firing order of the cylinders. Instead of taking chances, it is best to replace your spark plugs one at a time. After wiping off the engine block, place your spark plug socket over the spark plug, affix ratchet to socket and unscrew plug counter-clockwise. Remove from engine.

Pick up one of the new spark plugs and take a good look at it. For it to function properly, the gap between the electrodes at the wide end must match the specifications for your car. You can find those specifications in your owner's manual or on the engine plate under the hood.

Once you have found the proper gap, pick up the spark plug wire gauge and find the wire with the corresponding number. Slip it between the electrodes. If it moves too easily, the gap is too wide. Narrow it by gently pressing the outer electrode against a clean hard surface. If you are unable to get the wire between the electrodes because the gap is too narrow, use the part of the gauge designed for prying apart electrodes to set the gap properly. Properly means that the wire slides comfortably through the gap, just brushing against the electrodes.

Making sure there is no dirt which might fall into the hole, slip the gapped plug into the cylinder electrodes-first and tighten it with your fingers as much as you can. You always must begin tightening a spark plug by hand to avoid cross-threading it, which will render it useless. When the plug is as tight as you can make it by hand, attach the spark plug socket and ratchet handle and turn it gently until you have achieved a snug fit. Be careful not to twist it too tight or you will crack the plug's ceramic shell, which also makes it useless. The plug is in good and tight when it will no longer wiggle, but will unscrew with reasonable ease.

Now press the rubber boot of the spark plug wire firmly into place over the tip of the plug. Repeat the entire process until you have replaced all plugs.

Check your old plugs against the chart on the following page. They might provide you with an excellent clue to potential engine troubles.

SPARK PLUG CHECKLIST

PROBLEM	SYMPTOM	AILMENT AND CURE
Normal plug	Looks fine	Regap and re-install.
Worn-out plug	Electrodes worn down to the nub.	Outlived its usefulness. Replace.
Oil-fouled plug	Oily black deposits on center electrode.	Oil is leaking into cylinders. Replace plug. See mechanic about engine.
Carbon-fouled plug	Black soot on electrodes.	Air-fuel mixture is too rich, or too much stop-and-go driving. Replace plug, preferably with one that has higher heat range.
Lead-fouled plugs	Excessive light-colored deposits on electrodes.	Improper additives for your car in gas or oil. Switch to different brands till you find what works best. Replace plug.
Overheated plug.	Worn electrodes; blistered insulator.	Air-fuel mixture is too lean. Or manifold is leaking. Or timing is over-advanced. Or gap is too wide. Or heat range on plug is too hot. See mechanic.
High-speed glazing	Yellow-tan shiny deposit on electrode.	Engine temperature rose suddenly during hard acceleration and normal deposits could not chip off, but melted. Replace with plug in colder heat range.

A Line About Fuel

At its simplest, a carburetor is a metal container in which gasoline and air combine to form the highly explosive mixture which, ignited by the spark plugs, powers the engine. Under normal driving conditions, some 14 parts of air by weight and 9000 by volume are required for every part of gasoline that goes into the mixture. But, because driving conditions vary and mechanical devices somehow come unglued, your carburetor is equipped with adjusting controls. They are called the idle mixture adjusting screw, the idle speed screw and, on late model cars, the idle stop solenoid.

It is imperative that your carburetor always be properly adjusted. A lean air-fuel mixture, one in which there is too much air, will cause your car to idle rough and to hesitate during acceleration. A rich air-fuel mixture, in which there is too little air, will result in thick, dark exhaust emissions and poor gas mileage. If the idle speed is adjusted too high, the engine will continue to run and sputter even after the ignition is shut off, a phenomenon known as dieseling. If the idle speed is too low, the car probably will stall when you take your foot off the gas. All of these problems are easily remedied.

As its name implies, it is the idle mixture adjusting screw which regulates the air-fuel mixture. To make any necessary adjustments, set the parking brakes, switch on the engine and allow it to warm up. Then raise the hood and remove the air filter housing over the carburetor. (See illustration on next page.)

Locate the idle mixture adjusting screw on the carburetor and turn it inward until the engine sputters. Then turn it the other way until the engine begins running smoothly. If you continue too far, the engine

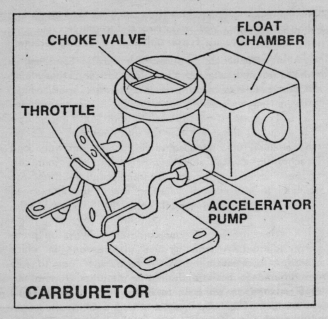

CHOKE VALVE

FLOAT CHAMBER

THROTTLE

ACCELERATOR PUMP

CARBURETOR

will sputter again as the result of a too rich air-fuel mixture, so be careful. When the engine is purring—stop. You have made the proper adjustment. Two-barrel and four-barrel carburetors are equipped with two idle mixture screws. Adjust them both according to the previous instructions.

To adjust your car's idle speed, you first must determine whether your car is equipped with an idle speed screw or an idle stop solenoid. If you are uncertain, check the owner's manual or the metal tune-up plate on the firewall under the hood. Check further to see if your car's idle speed should be adjusted with the air cleaner on or off the carburetor and also find out the correct idle speed, which will be listed in RPMs, or

Revolutions Per Minute. To obtain an RPM reading from your car's engine, you will need a tachometer.

Once you've located your idle speed screw, set the parking brake, turn on the ignition and allow the engine to warm up, so that the choke butterfly is fully open. Then kill the engine. If your manual tells you to remove the air filter, which it probably does, do so. Otherwise do not. In either case, the next step is to attach the tachometer to the engine. To do this, ground the black lead by affixing it to any metal part of the engine. Then connect the red lead to the ignition coil at the clamp which holds the wire leading to the distributor. Start up the engine again.

Compare the tachometer reading with the specifications in the owner's manual. If the numbers jibe, your job is over before it's really begun. If they do not, use a screwdriver to turn the idle speed screw until you achieve the proper reading. If your idle speed is low, turn the screw clockwise to increase the RPMs. If the speed is high, turn the screw counterclockwise, or outward, to decrease it. When the numbers match, shut off the engine, disconnect the tachometer, replace the air filter housing and test drive the car.

If your car is equipped with an idle stop solenoid, rather than an idle speed screw, check the metal plate for the adjustment specifications. Then set the parking brake, turn on the engine and run it long enough to warm it up. Turn off the engine, remove the air filter housing and attach the tachometer as described earlier. Start the engine again.

Compare the tachometer reading with the manufacturer's specification and, if any adjustment is necessary, use a wrench to turn the solenoid adjusting nut, clockwise to increase RPMs, counterclockwise to decrease them.

Now it is time to make what is known as the base

idle adjustment. Begin by disconnecting the solenoid wire at the connector. As the solenoid plunger retracts, the idle speed will drop.

The new RPM reading should be around 500, which is the reduced speed which allows your engine to stop running when the ignition is switched off. If you are not getting a reading in the neighborhood of 500, turn the idle speed screw until such a reading is reached.

Reconnect the solenoid wire and give the engine enough gas to increase the RPMs and allow the solenoid plunger to return to its initial position. When you cut back on the gas the tachometer reading should return to the specification for normal idling.

Shut off the engine, disconnect the tachometer, replace the air filter housing and test drive the car.

Climate helps dictate the air-fuel mixture your carburetor requires. A warm engine requires a leaner, more aerated mixture than a cold engine. To regulate the flow of air, all carburetors are equipped with a choke whose most important feature is a butterfly flap over the air horn. Most old-fashioned American cars and modern imported sports cars have manual chokes, while today's American cars have automatic chokes. In either case, it is essential that the butterfly flap function properly, moving from the closed position, which guarantees a richer mixture when the engine is cold, to an open position, which forces a leaner mixture after the engine has warmed up.

A stuck butterfly flap is no fun. If it is frozen in the open position it will be difficult to start your car on most days, impossible on cold days. If it is shut tight after the engine has started, the car will burn too much gas and emit clouds of black smoke.

To test for a stuck butterfly flap, allow the engine to cool off overnight. In the morning, raise the hood, remove the air cleaner and look inside the carburetor air horn. You will probably find the choke open.

Now get behind the car's wheel, or better yet have someone else do so, and hit the gas pedal. If the flap snaps shut, things are looking good. Start the engine and let it run for a couple of minutes. If the choke is in good shape, the butterfly flap will open again. If it does not, or if it never snapped shut in the first place, apply an automatic choke cleaner spray to the inside of the carburetor horn. Allow the liquid to soak in and then jiggle the butterfly flap with your fingers until it is moving freely. Wipe off the excess liquid with a clean rag and then have your assistant step on the gas. If the flap opens, everything is fine. If nothing happens, see a mechanic. The thermostatic coil may be broken.

Perched atop your car's cylinder head, toward the rear, is the PCV valve, the most visible component of the pollution fighting system. The initials PCV, contrary to popular belief, do not stand for pollution control valve, the system is made up of a return tube leading from the crankcase to the intake manifold whose purpose is to draw from the crankcase the gasoline combustion byproducts and noxious vapors which have leaked past the piston rings. These it disperses by feeding them back into the cylinders for reburning.

It is the job of the PCV valve to control the flow of air while the car is idling. As much as 25 percent of the air used during idling must flow through the valve. If your car idles rough, especially right after a tune-up, there is a good chance that the cause is a defective or clogged valve or tube. Other symptoms of a malfunctioning valve are the presence of smelling fumes in the passenger compartment and a steady drip of oil from the front and rear engine seals under the car.

If you suspect that your PCV valve needs replacing, shut off the ignition. When the engine is cold, raise the hood and find the thick hose on the air cleaner which leads toward the valve. Pull out the hose and shake it. If the valve rattles, the trouble is somewhere else. If the valve does not rattle, it is time to replace it. In either case, clean out the hose before doing anything else.

Remove the valve from the hose by unscrewing a clamp, or unscrewing the valve with an adjustable wrench, or in most cases merely by pulling it out by hand. Then insert a new valve or re-insert the old one after soaking it in carburetor cleaner. Replace the hose, tighten all clamps, if necessary, and lower the hood.

If your car seems to have lost its pep when you kick the accelerator hard and pull into the passing lane, the problem might be a clogged fuel filter. To prevent harmful contaminants from entering the carburetor, auto manufacturers have installed inline filters on their cars. As dirt accumulates in the filter, the flow of gas becomes restricted. Should a fuel filter be neglected for a very long time, it can become so clogged with dirt that no gas will reach the carburetor and the engine will not run. To prevent that from happening, you should replace your car's fuel filter every 12,000 miles.

In general, there are three different kinds of fuel filters. (See illustration opposite.) If you are driving a General Motors product, your car probably is equipped with a bronze or paper element filter housed just inside the carburetor inlet. To replace it, raise the hood and remove the air cleaner housing. Before disconnecting fuel line, ready a clean rag to absorb the gasoline that will spill out as you do. Then remove the large retaining nut, being careful not to lose the spring right behind the filter. Remove the spring and the filter

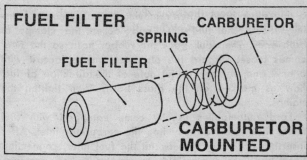

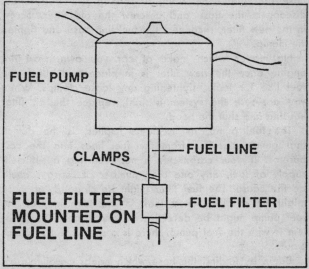

and then install the new filter. Replace the spring, tighten the retaining nut and reconnect the fuel line to the carburetor.

If your car was made by Chrysler or AMC, it probably has an in-line filter which looks something like

a tiny glass bowl. After removing the air cleaner housing, locate the fuel filter and loosen the clamps at
both ends. Then pull back the rubber hose so the filter
comes loose. Discard the old filter and replace it with
a new one, taking careful note of the direction of fuel
flow as marked on the glass bowl. Then tighten the
clamps.

Ford automobiles usually come equipped with fuel
filters that screw directly into the carburetor inlet. After
inserting a clean rag between the fuel filter, connecting
hose and intake manifold, to sop up spilled gasoline,
disconnect the hose and unscrew the old filter. Screw
in the new filter, reconnect the fuel line hose and tighten
the clamp.

No matter which make of car you own, start the
engine once the new filter is in place and check the
fuel line for leaks, tightening any loose clamps. When
you are sure the system is tight, replace the air filter
housing and shut the hood.

The fuel pump, as its name implies, is the device
that pumps gasoline from the fuel lines into the carburetor. If your carburetor is not receiving a sufficient
supply of fuel, any one of a number of reasons could
be the cause. The fuel filter might be clogged, or there
might be a block or a leak in the fuel line, or the
fuel pump might be defective. If you suspect the problem is with the fuel pump, there is a simple test to check
it out.

Begin by finding the hose which brings gasoline from
the fuel pump to the carburetor. Disconnect it near
the carburetor and attach it to a long length of hose
emptying into a jar or a can. Have someone get inside
your car and start the engine. If gasoline comes out
of the hose, the pump probably is doing its job. If not,
see a mechanic.

Get the Greasies

It doesn't hurt, every 6000 miles or so, to repack your outer front wheel bearing in fresh grease. As does everything else on your car, grease wears out. Sometimes it dries out. Other times it liquifies, becoming too thin to properly lubricate the bearings. If not replaced promptly, the results may be disastrous, because bearings are precision parts.

For this messy, but relatively simply, task you should come equipped with a can of long fiber wheel bearing grease, a tire jack, cutting pliers, slip joint pliers, a new cotter pin and some rags. Those of you with tender joints might also consider the use of knee pads.

Following the tire-changing instructions in Chapter 2, remove the hubcap from the left front wheel, loosen the lug nuts, jack up the car and slip off the tire. Remove the dust cap from the wheel hub with the slip joint pliers and use the cutting pliers to remove the cotter pin from the spindle nut. Unscrew the spindle nut by turning it counterclockwise and remove it, too. (See illustration on next page.)

Now tug at the brake drum until it moves a few inches toward you. By pushing it back in place, you will bring out the washer and outer wheel bearings. With the washer still in front, slide the bearings off the spindle and examine them. If you see flecks of metal in the grease, the bearings are worn and should be replaced. If not, wrap the washers and bearings in a rag to prevent dust and dirt from getting at them.

Now you are ready to take the brake drum off the spindle by pulling it toward you. When you have removed it, place it flat on the ground, face upward, and wipe away all excess grease from the spindle

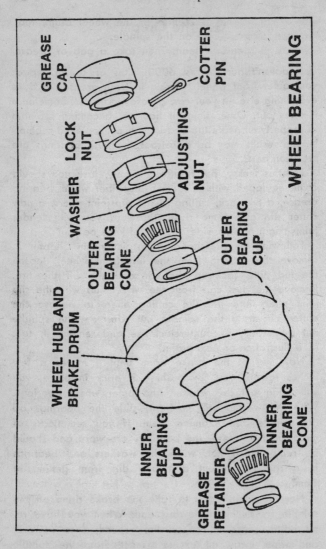

WHEEL BEARING

GREASE CAP

COTTER PIN

LOCK NUT

WASHER

ADJUSTING NUT

OUTER BEARING CONE

OUTER BEARING CUP

WHEEL HUB AND BRAKE DRUM

INNER BEARING CUP

INNER BEARING CONE

GREASE RETAINER

with a rag. Clean the center of the wheel drum, too, and replace the wheel on the spindle.

Wipe the bearing clean. Then take a gob of grease in one hand and press the bearing into it, forcing the grease all over. Then, narrow end first, replace the bearing on the spindle and follow it by replacing the washer.

Put the spindle nut back on the spindle, tighten it and then unscrew it one full notch. Make sure it lines up with the hole in the spindle by turning it to the left. Insert a new cotter pin, bending one of the legs and pressing it flat against the nut. Snip off the other leg with cutting pliers. Replace dust cap, tighten lug nuts and bang hub cap back into place. Lower car, then repeat process on the other wheels.

It is wise to change your oil every 4000 miles; 3000 if you really love your car. For older cars, or cars subjected to stop and go driving, a longer wait between oil changes may prove fatal.

Check your owner's manual, or the next section of this chapter, to find out what type of oil your car requires. Most newer cars are designed to use multi-viscosity oil, which will not thicken in cold weather or thin out during hot weather driving. In addition to the oil, probably about five quarts' worth, you will also need to buy a new oil filter, oil drain plug gasket, oil filter wrench, an oil can spout (or beer can opener) and an old basin or oil-drainer-container. The latter is a large plastic can with two caps—one on the side with which to collect the used oil and the other, on the top, to pour it out.

Warm the engine so that the old oil and all the dirt it contains will flow freely, but not so hot that it will burn you when you touch it.

After shutting off the engine, locate the oil pan at the bottom of the crankcase and touch the oil drain plug under the pan. If it is not too hot to work with go back to your tool kit and find the wrench you will need to loosen it. If the plug is not easily accessible, you will have to get under the car. Do not jack up the car, because if the front end is raised the oil may not drain completely out of the oil pan.

Before unscrewing the plug, make certain your basin or your drainer-container is in position underneath. Loosen the plug until it is just about ready to come out, but don't remove it yet. To avoid an oil spill along your arm and sleeve, use a rag to grab the plug and give it the final turn out of the pan. Then get your hand out of the way.

Don't worry if the plug falls into the basin and is lost in a sea of filthy oil. You fish it out later, after all the oil is in the pan. In the meantime, go back to your toolkit and get the oil filter wrench.

You should not have any trouble locating your oil filter. Sticking out of the side of your engine at a sharp angle, it resembles a tin can, which more or less is what it is. Probably you can loop the wrench around the filter merely by reaching for it. However, if the filter is accessible only from underneath, you're going to have to jack up the car after all. In either event, unscrew it with the wrench and dispose of it gingerly. Remember, it is filled with dirty oil. (See illustration on opposite page.)

Lubricate the gasket on the open end of your new oil filter with a dab of oil and after all the oil is out of the crankcase screw the filter onto the engine. Although a snug fit is essential, do not use the oil filter wrench. Tightening the new filter too much may cause it to bend and leak.

Use another rag to clean the area where the oil drain plug will be reinserted. Before replacing the plug, check to see if the old gasket looks healthy. If it does not, scrape it off the oil pan with a screwdriver and install a new one before replacing the plug.

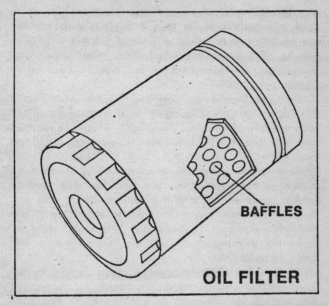

BAFFLES

OIL FILTER

Open all five cans of oil with the oil can spout or can opener and then remove the breather cap from the top of the engine. Install the oil into the crankcase through the filler hole. Check the dipstick with one can remaining and add just enough to bring the level up to "full."

Put the breather cap back on the cylinder head and then start your engine, keeping an eye on the dashboard. In about a quarter of a minute, the red "idiot" light should go out as oil pressure is restored in the crankcase. If the light remains on, kill the engine and check the dipstick. If it reads "low," tread cautiously. You probably forgot to replace the oil drain plug in the pan.

If the light goes out and no problems arise, check

the dipstick a second time after allowing the car to cool off. Don't worry if the oil level appears to have dropped, because about a pint of the lubricant now should be inside the new oil filter. Install enough oil to get the level indicated on the dipstick back up to "full."

Put your tools away now and dispose of the used oil. You might try offering it to a neighborhood gas station. They often save "drippings," which are recycled into low grade lubricants when passed on to oil reclaimers.

As a rule, it is best to select a quality, brand name motor oil for your engine the first time you need to add a quart and stick with it for the life of your car. But, as you travel down that long, lonely highway, it is inevitable that your dipstick is going to read "add one" when the only brands on sale are nothing you've ever heard of before.

To give you an idea of what you're getting in that can with the strange label, the Society of Automotive Engineers (SAE) has come up with a classification code for automotive oil. Usually, the specification is printed on the label or stamped into the can. This is what the SAE is trying to tell you:

SA—Utility Gasoline. The cheapest kind available and affording your engine minimal protection against friction. Try never to use it.

SB—Minimum Duty Gasoline. Not much more expensive than SA, nor much better.

SC—1964 Gasoline Engine Warranty Maintenance Service. This grade of oil meets the needs of most cars and trucks manufactured between 1964 and 1967, but the longevity of some of those vehicles should not be regarded as a testament to its value. This stuff can be used without worry in cars of mid 60s vintage, but generally should be avoided if intended for use in new cars.

SD—1968 Gasoline Engine Warranty Maintenance Service. A marked improvement over the lower grades, this oil will not harm cars of 1971 vintage. Older cars may thrive on it, but newer cars will rebel at a steady diet.

SE—1972 Gasoline Engine Warranty Maintenance Service. Simply the best. Designed to provide new cars with maximum protection against high temperature engine deposits, rust, corrosion and oil oxidation. It costs a bit more than the next highest brand, but is cheaper in the long run if you care about maximizing the life of your engine.

Motor oils also are graded according to viscosity, or ability to pour, in a system in which the higher numbers refer to heavier, thicker oils. If you are driving a car with an engine that already has rolled up a lot of miles, it would be best to stick to a heavy grade of oil. Lighter-weighted oil probably would seep past the worn piston rings, leaving the engine unprotected. However, heavier grades of oil are not the solution to all lubrication problems because the stuff does not run enough on very cold winter days.

Drivers of newer cars can avoid problems by installing multi-viscosity oils containing additives that help the engine achieve year-round lubricating capabilities—not thinning out too much in summer, nor congealing in winter. A good grade of multi-viscosity motor oil for a fairly new car is 10W—40. Still other additives may prevent engine corrosion, reduce friction between moving metal parts, prevent foaming at high temperatures, loosen slude and help keep the engine clean.

Although the latter sounds so good that you may

wonder why every motorist doesn't install it in his engine right away, there is a very good reason why
"detergent" motor oils might not be best for you. If
your car's engine has logged many thousands of miles,
it probably has built up a large deposit of sludge which
has found a comfortable place for itself, out of harm's
way, somewhere in your crankcase. Should you suddenly
shock your aging engine by treating it to a detergent
motor oil, you may succeed in dislodging this sludge,
circulating it through the engine and quite literally gum-
ming up the works.

Although non-professional mechanics should keep
their hands off their car's transmission, there is no
reason for anyone not to be able to check and install
transmission fluid. Begin by locating the transmission
fluid dipstick handle at the rear of the engine. Make
certain that you do not confuse it with the oil dipstick.

Although an oil dipstick should be checked with a
cold engine, transmission fluid should be checked while
the engine is at normal operating temperature and the
car is in parking gear. Simply pull out the dipstick, wipe
it with a clean lint-free rag, place it all the way back in
the engine and pull it out again. If the reading indicates
that you are low on fluid—which may account for why
your transmission is making all that noise and is so hard
to shift into gear—buy the proper transmission fluid
and install it through a funnel into the same hole from
which you removed the dipstick. It is impossible to stress
enough the importance of buying the correct fluid.
Consult your owner's manual before laying out any cash.
If the manual is not available, check with the service
department manager at the local dealer who sells your
make of car.

That's the Brakes

You can't be too careful with your car's brakes. At least once a year, or every 12,000 miles, it is imperative that you get inside your car's brake drums and check the parts for signs of wear. If you're too lazy to inspect all four brakes, the least you should do is inspect one front and one rear brake. Three fairly distinct procedures are involved in inspecting front drum brakes, rear drum brakes and front disc brakes. But all begin the same way —with the engine shut off, the emergency brake set (a must for any brake job, don't forget) the hubcaps removed and the lugnuts loosened.

Front Drum Brakes

Take a look at the previous chapter and follow the instructions for inspecting your car's outer wheel bearings. After removing the bearings, grab the brake drum and slide it off the spindle with the inner bearings still inside. (See illustration on page 42.) If there is an air gun handy, this is a good time to clean both the inside and outside of the drum. Do not inhale any of the dust; it contains large quantities of asbestos fibers, a potential cancer-causing agent. If an air gun is not available, an old paint brush, a clean rag or a vacuum cleaner are just about as good and they stir up a lot less dust.

Now take a look inside the brake drum. If you find deep grooves or cracks or burned spots in the inner walls, the drums should be resurfaced by a mechanic. Check the wheel cylinder on the brake backing plate for signs of leaking—another matter for a trained mechanic. Then inspect the brake linings. Healthy linings are evenly worn and have no thin spots. If the

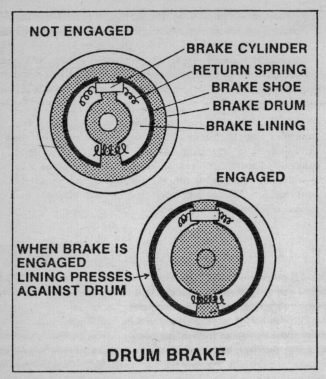

NOT ENGAGED

BRAKE CYLINDER
RETURN SPRING
BRAKE SHOE
BRAKE DRUM
BRAKE LINING

ENGAGED

WHEN BRAKE IS
ENGAGED
LINING PRESSES
AGAINST DRUM

DRUM BRAKE

lining is riveted, the rivet heads should not come above the surface of the lining. Bonded linings should have a minimal thickness of 1/16 of an inch. If the linings are worn, have a mechanic replace them. Finally, examine all springs, cables and self-adjusting devices. A mechanic will have to be the one to fix any that are broken.

It is time now to close up the patient. Replace the brake drum and outer wheel bearings and then slip the washer over the axle spindle. Follow the remainder of the procedure described in the section on checking outer wheel bearings. Check the brakes on the other front wheel.

Front Disc Brakes

With the parking brake on, the car jacked up and the wheel off, examine the surfaces of both sides of the disc (see illustration), paying special attention to uneven wear and rust. If you find either, or cracks, or grooves, or excessive wear, see a mechanic. Now look at the brake pads. Uneven or worn linings (less than a 1/16 of an inch thick) will have to be replaced by

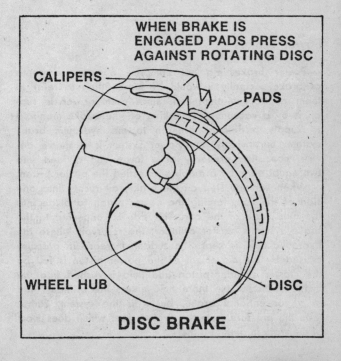

WHEN BRAKE IS ENGAGED PADS PRESS AGAINST ROTATING DISC

CALIPERS

PADS

WHEEL HUB

DISC

DISC BRAKE

a mechanic. Also check the pads on both sides of the rotor.

Now replace the wheel on the spindle, tighten the lug nuts, lower the car and put back the hubcaps. Check the brakes on the other front wheel.

Rear Drum Brakes

To inspect rear drum brakes, follow the procedure set for front drum brakes. The job will be a bit simpler, because there aren't any outer wheel bearings to contend with.

Power Brakes

Power brakes do not comprise a separate genus of brake. Actually it would be more fitting to refer to them as vacuum-enhanced, since their power is supplied by a vacuum unit working off the intake manifold to supply additional strength to the hydraulic brake system. Surprisingly, the power system is a simple device, consisting primarily of a large can divided into two equal parts by a diaphragm called the power piston. Whenever you step on the brake, air rushes into one side of the can, forcing the power piston to bulge into the other side of the can. This side is connected to the brake system's master cylinder, the reservoir where the hydraulic fluid is kept. The sudden increase in pressure caused by the movement of the power piston is felt by the master cylinder piston and fluid is rushed into the brake cylinders. No more fluid enters the cylinder than in a conventional brake, but it is the system, rather than the pressure from the driver's foot which does most of the work in getting it there.

A grand idea, you say? Not bad—but there is one drawback. When the power system fails, which it sometimes does, it requires every bit of a motorist's strength to get the car to stop. Some drivers report that they found themselves standing on the brake pedal when their car finally came to a halt. Instead of having to resort to such acrobatics to bring your car to a stop in an emergency, check your power brake system periodically.

Shut off the engine and pump the brake pedal a few times, until you have filled the vacuum in the power brake system. As you do, you should notice a marked increase in the pressure required for the brakes to catch. If you don't, there is something wrong. The question is whether it is inside or outside the power system.

To find out, start up the engine while the brake pedal is depressed. The pedal should move downward if the vacuum system is working. If it does not, the power breaking system is leaking. See a mechanic.

Another part of your car's brake system which requires periodic inspection is the master cylinder, where the hydraulic brake fluid is stored. In some cars, the master cylinder resembles a small plastic container with a screw-on cap. More commonly, it is a cast iron container mounted under the hood against the fire wall. To get a look at its contents you'll have to pry off the clamp which secures the lid. Never, we repeat, begin any job on your brake system without first setting the emergency brake.

As you remove the lid, make sure that no dirt or grease falls into the cylinder. Now take a look inside. The fluid in each chamber should reach to within a third of an inch of the top. If it is low, add the proper hydraulic brake fluid for your car's system. Then replace the lid and fasten the clamp.

Before shutting the hood, check for signs of a master

cylinder leak under the cylinder and on the firewall. If you find any traces of brake fluid, take your car to a mechanic. If your mechanic puts your car on a lift, check for leaks in the brake lines by tracking the lines from each wheel to the engine.

If it feels like you're stepping on cheese, or a wet sponge whenever you hit your brake pedal, it's time to bleed your brakes. This procedure will not leave them mortally wounded. It will cure them—of air bubbles in the brake fluid which may have entered during repairs, or through a leak in the system.

Shut off the engine, block the rear wheels, jack up the front end and locate the brake bleeder nozzle behind all four brakes. (See illustration on opposite page.) Then use an ignition (or box-end) wrench to open and immediately close each of the nozzles about half a turn. Don't worry if a small amount of fluid seeps out. This is to be expected.

Now that all four nozzles are loosened, place the wrench over one of them. Don't turn it yet. Instead, attach a small piece of rubber hose to the nozzle and insert the other end of the hose in a clean jar containing a few inches of brake fluid.

Have an assistant get inside the car and pump the brake pedal. While he is holding down the pedal, open the nozzle. As brake fluid containing air bubbles fills the air, his foot will go down to the floorboards. Have him hold it there until you have tightened the nozzle. If he releases the pedal too soon, air will be drawn back into the system and you will have wasted your time and effort.

Now open the master cylinder and refill it. This will prevent all fluid from draining out of the cylinder and air from being sucked into the brake system. After refilling the cylinder, drain the other three brakes in the same manner as you drained the first.

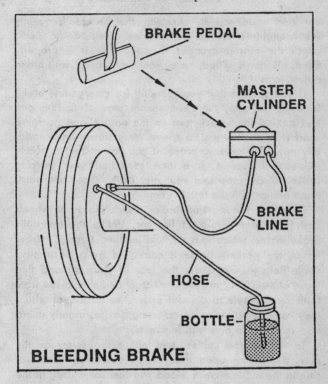

BLEEDING BRAKE

After draining the fourth brake, re-fill the master cylinder again. Don't use the fluid just drained out of the system. It may be contaminated. If at any time you drain all the fluid out of the master cylinder, you will have to bleed the cylinder in much the same way as you bled the brakes. Do this by removing all the fluid from the cylinder at the spot where the brake lines connect to the cylinder. Again, use your jar to collect what little fluid remains.

In either event, after completing the job, lower the

car and road test it, checking the brakes frequently for sponginess. If the pedal goes down to the floor, check the master cylinder to make sure it is properly filled. If it is filled, see your mechanic for brake adjustments.

If you suspect that your parking (or emergency) brake is losing its grip, there's a simple way of finding out. Get behind the wheel, turn on the engine and go for a short ride at a very slow speed. Very slowly and gradually apply the parking brake. If you do not feel a steady decrease in speed, it is time to adjust your parking brake. If you know that your rear brake shoes are worn, don't bother with the test. It's time.

To adjust the parking brake, block the front wheels and jack up the rear of the car. Unlike the hydraulic brake system which runs on fluid pumped through rubber hoses, the parking brake is controlled by a mechanical cable linkage. Get under the rear of your car and find those cables. They are made of steel and should run from both rear wheels to a point under the back seat where they come together at an adjusting device, usually a bar and screw, or a bolt with lock nuts.

To tighten the cables, turn either the screw or the nuts, depending upon your car's equipment, until tension in the cable increases and you feel some drag in the rear wheels when you spin them by hand. Then loosen them enough for the drag to disappear. This should be the ideal adjustment, so tighten the screw or the nuts and go for another test drive. The brake now should be so tight that it is virtually impossible to drive the car with the emergency brake fully set.

It is extremely important that the parking brake not be set too tight. If it is, you will wear out your brake shoes in no time, as well as put a dangerous strain on your engine.

Cooling It—Part 1

When you consider that temperatures inside your engine may reach 4500 degrees Fahrenheit under normal driving conditions, it is no wonder that the cooling system is considered one of your car's unsung heroes. Because it responds so well to the incredible demands made upon it—and rarely fails—it is also one of the most overlooked areas of your car. But neglect is not a diet on which it will thrive forever. A simple check conducted every three or four months will help locate impending trouble before it becomes serious. And make no mistake about it, cooling system problems can be a portent of disaster. Without proper cooling, the heat generated by an internal combustion engine could melt your engine block in less than half an hour.

It is unforgivable to drive off in the morning without glancing under your car to see which vital fluids might have leaked out overnight. Often you will find a trace of oil, which you can forget about. A pink, greasy substance under the engine is transmission fluid. If the puddle is rusty brown, or green, it is probably anti-freeze and it is time to take a long, hard look at your cooling system (See illustration on next page.)

Check all hoses while the engine is still cold, squeezing and flexing them to test the condition of the rubber. Hoses feel firm and resilient when they are in good shape and snap back into shape after being squeezed. If any of your engine's hoses feel soft, or if they are hard and brittle, or contain bulges, replace them right away. Do the same if they are cracked and leaking, or are marked with whitish deposits at the source of old leaks. If you have a hose more than 25,000 miles old, replace it, too.

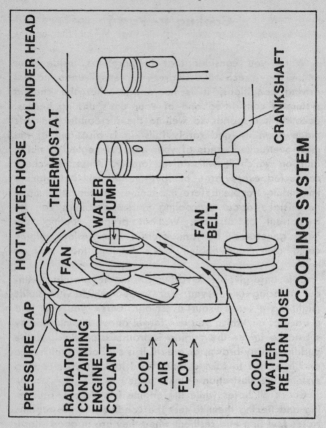

COOLING SYSTEM

A healthy radiator cap is another essential for efficient cooling. **When checking the radiator cap, always make sure the engine is cold.** Because the coolant inside the radiator is under high pressure, it may spurt out of the system and scald you should you remove the radiator cap when the engine still is hot. Even if your car's radiator cap is equipped with a pressure release valve, it is best to let the engine cool.

When you remove the cap, check the inside for a cracked rubber seal and rust. Either one means it is time to replace the cap. Before you buy, make sure you are getting the proper size replacement.

Small circular depressions on both sides of the engine block, called freeze plugs, also are potential trouble spots. Most engines contain at least seven of the plugs, which serve no other purpose than to fill up holes that were made when the block was cast at the foundry. Rust streaks around the plugs are a sure sign that there is a leak. If you catch it quickly enough, you might be able to solve the problem with a sealant. Otherwise, see your mechanic. Insist that he replace the faulty plug with a brass one, which won't rust.

Still another source of cooling system leaks is a faulty water pump. Mounted behind the fan belt pulley, it can be checked simply by shaking the fan when the engine is off and listening for a rattle. If you hear such a noise, or detect a side-to-side movement of the fan and pulley, the pump bearings are loose. It is also a good idea to check for moisture at the small vent hole at the bottom of the pump behind the fan pulley. If you find a leak there, have a mechanic replace the pump.

Don't forget to check the head gasket between the cylinder head and the engine block. Any trace of coolant residue there, see your mechanic.

Not to be overlooked, too, is the petcock, the tiny drain at the bottom of the radiator. Check it first by hand and, if you feel a few drops of moisture, make sure it is tightly shut. If the petcock has been damaged or moisture is seeping through the threads install a new one.

The most obvious place to look for leaks in your cooling system is in the radiator. Check for the whitish deposits or rust-colored stains indicating old leaks that already have dried. Look especially for seepage on both sides of the fins. A good sealant may satisfy this problem for a while, but, eventually, you will have to see a mechanic. The same holds true if you find the radiator leaking badly when you check it. Radiator work is *expensive* work, most often, and you always get a written estimate before letting anyone touch it.

If your examination of the cooling system ends up negative, but your car continues to lose liquid from the radiator, try and get your hands on a "cooling system pressure tester." This is a small, hand-operated pump which you fit over the radiator filler hole when the engine is cold. As you pump air into the cooling system, check the attached gauge until it reaches the pressure level at which, according to your owner's manual, your cooling system is designed to operate. Ideally, the pressure should hold for up to half an hour. But if there are leaks anywhere in the system, the needle on the gauge will drop. In some cases, liquid will seep out of the leaky spot and hoses will bulge where they are weak. If the pressure test fails to turn up any indication of a leak, replace the radiator cap from the pressure tester with your car's regular radiator cap. The gauge will show whether your cap can take the pressure under which your cooling system must operate. If it can't, buy a new cap.

Forget anything you may have heard about "permanent" anti-freeze. There ain't no such animal. At least once a year, usually in the late autumn or early spring, you should drain your car's radiator and install new anti-freeze. This also is the best time to flush the radiator and cooling system, purging it of the rust and sludge which accumulate in the normal course of driving.

You may get away with not flushing your cooling system for a year or two, but, in time, the accumulation of rust will catch up with you, clogging the narrow channels in your radiator. When enough of the channels are gummed up—and enough is a surprisingly small amount—the remaining open channels will not be sufficient for dispersing all the heat generated by the engine. And you quite literally may find yourself in hot water.

Begin with the engine cold and the ignition off. Raise the hood and remove the radiator cap by turning it counter-clockwise. Then reach under the radiator and locate the petcock—the winged nut on the bottom. Use your pliers to turn the petcock to the left until it screws out of the radiator and then get out of the way of the rusty water. If you've dropped the petcock, don't be in a hurry to retrieve it. It's not going anywhere.

Instead, while the water is draining out of the radiator, look for the engine petcock. On a six-cylinder car it usually is located on the side opposite the carburetor. V-8 cars generally have two engine petcocks—one on each side. Twist the petcocks to the left until they are wide open and let the coolant pour out.

When the cooling system has drained, replace the petcock and pour a can of chemical flush in the radiator. Then fill the radiator with water from a garden hose, replace the radiator cap and start the engine. After letting it run for about a quarter of an hour, shut it off, drain the cooling system again, remove the radiator cap, place the garden hose in the filler neck and turn on the water. Keep the water running until no traces of rust are visible in the water running out of the radiator. Shut off the hose, allow all the water to drain out of the cooling system and tighten the petcock with pliers.

Now you are ready to install the anti-freeze. In most parts of the country, a 50-50 mixture of anti-freeze and water is recommended, although in colder areas a stronger solution may be preferred. In any case, check the chart on the side of the anti-freeze container to find the ideal mixture for your car. Install the anti-freeze first, then add water.

Once the anti-freeze has been installed, start the engine and then get back to the radiator to monitor the coolant level. As it drops, begin adding water. Don't stop until the level reaches a spot about an inch below the filler neck. Then replace the radiator cap and shut the hood.

Most modern cooling systems call for an even mixture of anti-freeze and water. Too much water often leads to overheating in the summer. Should the coolant become extremely diluted, freezing and the attendant danger of a cracked engine block become genuine winter hazards. To test the percentage of anti-freeze—or at least its ethylene glycol base—in the fluid in your cooling system, you will need a hydrometer very similar to the one used to check battery fluid.

To be certain the coolant is properly mixed, always perform your anti-freeze check with the engine running. If your car just has overheated and you are wondering why, don't rush into things. Wait a minimum of a quarter of an hour for your engine to cool off before unscrewing the radiator cap. Remember that you run the risk of scalding yourself any time you remove the radiator cap from a hot engine.

Check the level of the coolant to make certain it is an inch below the filler neck. If it appears to be reddish brown and opaque, proceed no further with your test. What you are looking at is a rusty solution which requires immediate flushing and replacement. If the coolant is clear, start the engine again and suck some fluid into the hydrometer by squeezing the rubber bulb and releasing it.

Make sure there is enough fluid in the glass tube for the little balls to float. Then compare the reading against the chart on the hydrometer which tells you the degree of protection afforded by the mixture.

If the chart says that you have protection to 20 below zero, empty the hydrometer back into the radiator, reinstall the pressure cap and forget about it. If you live in International Falls, Minn., or someplace with a comparable Arctic-like climate, however, you should guarantee protection all the way down to 34 below zero.

Do so by shutting off the engine, opening the radiator petcock and draining off about two quarts of fluid. Replace with two quarts of anti-freeze. If the hydrometer reading was between 19 below and ten above you will probably have to replace a gallon of fluid with anti-freeze for maximum protection. If the reading was above plus 11 degrees, drain all the coolant and install a 50-50 mixture of water and anti-freeze.

Perhaps the most vulnerable part of your car's cooling system are the five rubber hoses which funnel water in and out of the radiator and engine block. They are the upper and lower radiator hoses, the inlet and outlet heater hoses and the bypass hose for the water pump. Fortunately, they also are among the easiest and least expensive parts of your car to replace. Because all radiator and heater hoses can be expected to have a similar life expectancy—about three years—it is a good idea to replace all of them whenever one wears out. Here is how:

Start by draining the cooling system, preferably into a container with a five-gallon capacity since you will want to reinstall the same fluid later. Then examine the hose clamps. Basically three varieties—gear-type, screw-type and wire hose clamps. To remove the wire hose clamps you will need a pair of wire hose clamps pliers, which have a slit on the inside of each jaw to grip the end of the clamp. Gear-type clamps are the simplest of the three to work with and can be removed with a screwdriver. Screw-type clamps are a little more trouble. After completely unscrewing the screw, insert screwdriver under the clamp to loosen it.

After loosening the clamp of whatever type, slide it out of the way and then twist the hose to snap it out of the fittiing. If it has become fused with the metal, cut a five-inch lengthwise section with a knife and pry it away with a screwdriver. Scrape away or sand off whatever crud you find on the fitting.

To save yourself a lot of work, make replacements with "preformed" hose, which comes already fitted with the proper bend. If you are replacing a bottom radiator hose, specify you want a wire-reinforced hose. An enclosed wire coil helps the hose retain its shape in the vacuum formed when coolant is sucked out of the radiator by the water pump.

If the hose you are replacing carries liquid under pressure, smear gasket sealer over the fitting before installing the new one. Always remember to slip any new clamps over the hose before attaching it to the fitting. Once the new hose is in place, adjust the new hose clamps and tighten. Pour coolant back into radiator and check level. If you lost some fluid when you removed the hose in the first place, replace with anti-freeze or water before replacing radiator cap.

With the car in parking gear, start the engine and allow it to reach normal operating temperature. Check hose leakage and that clamps are tight.

Cooling It—Part 2

Another common source of annoying overheating problems is the thermostat. Essentially, the function of this temperature-sensitive valve is to keep the coolant in the engine block and out of the radiator long enough for the engine to warm up. As engine temperatures rise, the thermostat gradually opens to allow increasing amounts of coolant into the radiator. Proper operating temperature is fundamental to high performance, so the importance of the thermostat to your car cannot be overstated.

Should your car's thermostat lock in the closed position, coolant will be prevented from reaching the radiator and overheating will result. If, on the other hand, it refuses to close, the coolant will rush in and out of the radiator so fast that it will be difficult for the engine to warm up. Also, your car's heater will be useless on the coldest winter days when you need it the most.

A thermostat is a cheap little gadget, rarely exceeding $5 in cost, and easy to install. Begin by raising the hood and locating the thermostat. On most cars, the best place to look is where the top radiator hose meets the engine block, although on some models it is located in the bottom radiator hose. (See illustration on next page.)

While you drain the radiator to remove coolant from the thermostat housing, unscrew the radiator hose clamp and pull off the hose. Then remove the bolts which hold the housing to the engine block and take out the thermostat. Don't forget to remove the gasket as well, scraping away all the fragments. Prevent them from falling into the hole by stuffing a rag inside before you begin scraping.

Install the new thermostat in its place in the engine block, making certain that there is a snug fit. If there is not, you probably bought the wrong thermostat. Be sure the spring and actuator are pointing down into the engine and away from the radiator. Then smear

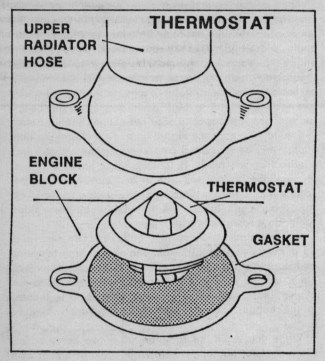

THERMOSTAT

UPPER
RADIATOR
HOSE

ENGINE
BLOCK

THERMOSTAT

GASKET

both sides of the new gasket with sealing compound and slip it over the thermostat onto the engine block. Replace the housing, tighten the bolts and attach the hose and clamps. Then refill the radiator and screw on the pressure cap.

Before admiring the results of your job, start the engine and allow it to run about a quarter of an hour. Then check for leaks around the thermostat housing and radiator hose. If you find any, look for loose connections and tighten them. Otherwise, just allow the engine to cool and check the level of the fluid in the radiator. If it is low, add some.

If your car continues to overheat, the result might be vapor lock, which is a fancy way of saying that your engine is running so hot the gasoline is boiling, or vaporizing, in the fuel line. Gas bubbles prevent the car's fuel pump from moving gasoline to the carburetor and, since an engine can't run with its fuel supply cut off, it stalls. The cure for the problem is to cool off the fuel pump and the fuel line.

Begin by raising the hood and removing the air cleaner housing. Then shine a flashlight into the throat of the carburetor and move the throttle linkage forward and backward. If you notice gasoline inside the carburetor, the vapor lock already may be broken, in which case you stand a good chance of starting your car by turning the key and keeping the gas pedal on the floor.

If you do not see any gasoline, find the fuel pump by backtracking along the large tube entering the carburetor. When you find the fuel pump, wrap some water-soaked rags around it. That should cool the fuel line sufficiently for you to be able to start your car within five minutes. If you don't have any water or rags with you when vapor lock strikes, all you can do is sit tight and wait it out. A half an hour with the engine shut off should do the trick.

Vapor lock usually is a symptom of chronic overheating, which may have a number of causes. It may begin with a frayed or loose fan belt, which is not strong enough to drive your water pump to capacity. The fault may lie with the bottom radiator hose, which sometimes collapses as a result of the vacuum caused by the action of the water pump, impeding the flow of coolant. Check it visually, with the engine on and the car in parking gear. If the hose has collapsed, install a new one.

Another clue to chronic overheating is your oil dipstick. If your car is running low on oil, engine friction is increasing. Also, oil normally is responsible for dispersing much of the heat in your engine as it flows into the crankcase.

Another possibility is that your radiator is so clogged that chemical flush is powerless to help you. If you suspect that is the case, take your car to a radiator shop where they will remove the radiator and steam clean the inside.

If even that fails, the only remedy may be to replace the radiator with a larger one that has an increased cooling capacity. Radical therapy indeed! But cheaper than buying a new car.

As your engine heats up, the pressure in the cooling system naturally rises. If it becomes greater than the level your radiator cap can handle, it will have to find an outlet. All cooling systems come equipped with such a safety valve in the form of the overflow pipe near the radiator filler hole. In cars which tend to overheat, coolant will escape through the overflow pipe almost every time they are driven. Since it is not a good idea to operate your car when the cooling system is not properly filled and since anti-freeze is too expensive and too much of a bother to install each and every time you want to use your car, someone came up with the clever idea of a coolant recovery system.

The components that go into a coolant recovery system are nothing more than a plastic container, or reservoir sealed with a cap from which two small rubber hoses extend. These items can be purchased inexpensively at any auto supply store in a kit costing less than five dollars, which also includes a new radiator cap.

To install the system, attach the bracket holding the reservoir to the frame of your car somewhere below the top of the overflow pipe. Then attach one of the hoses in the reservoir cap to the overflow pipe and replace the old radiator cap with the new one. The next time your cooling system overheats, the coolant will not be lost through the overflow pipe but will drain into the reservoir instead. Later, when the engine has cooled and the pressure inside the cooling system drops, the fluid will be drawn back into the radiator. Should so much coolant boil out of the radiator that not even the reservoir can hold it all, the second little hose functions as an overflow pipe for the reservoir.

That persistent rattling in the front of your engine might be the only warning you're ever going to get that your water pump's days are numbered. To find out if it's time to replace it, check visually for leaks and then shake the fan to see if you can make it rattle. Otherwise, take off the fan belt, which powers the pump, and run the engine to see if the noise is gone. If any of the tests turn up positive, you will have to replace the water pump.

Admittedly, this job is no fun. But it seems a lot more intimidating than it really is. Begin it by draining your radiator and removing the fan belt and all the hoses leading to and from the pump. Probably there are three of them in your car—the lower radiator hose, the bypass hose and the heater hose—and you should label each so that you will remember where to put it later.

Remove the bolts securing the fan to the water pump and then the bolts that hold the pump in place. Remove the water pump next and then scrape the gasket from the engine block, placing a clean rag in the hole to keep any dirt from falling inside. When the mounting surface is clean, apply a water resistant sealing compound to both sides of the new gasket and place it in position on the engine block.

Install the new pump so that it fits over the gasket and then replace the mounting bolts. Now put back the fan, hoses and fan belt and re-fill the radiator. Then start the engine and take a spin around the block. When you get back to your garage, hunt for leaks and make any necessary adjustments.

The forgotten part of your car's cooling system is the heater, which can be used to provide an important outlet for the heat which builds up during stop and go driving. Although the heater usually is one of the most trouble-free parts of your car, it, too, is subject to occasional troubles. One of the more common is a failure to supply sufficient heat.

Since your car's heater operates on the heat developed by the engine, do not expect to feel a rush of warm air the instant that you switch on the ignition. However, if you have been driving for a quarter of an hour or so with the heater knob in the "hot" position and feel nothing when you turn on the fan, then the heater is broken and the cause is probably a loose, or disconnected cable. You will have to reconnect the heater knob cable to the water valve—a procedure which also will solve the problem of a heater which will not shut off the flow of warm air.

Slither down on the floor in front of the passenger's seat, so that you are looking up under the dashboard. With one hand, slide the heater knob on the dash from one end to the other and, with your other hand, find the cable beginning behind the heater knob. At the end of the cable you will find a small loop on a thin wire which slides inside a metal sheath. Nearby, on the engine wall, is a small lever with a tiny metal tip. What has happened is that the loop has slipped out of the tip. Replace the loop and then slide the heater knob from one end to the other again, this time making certain that the little lever is moving. If it is, climb back up to the driver's seat, start the engine, run it for a quarter of an hour and switch on the heater fan. Soon you will know whether your heater is working again.

If you feel warm air drifting out from under the dashboard, but the fan will not operate, the problem probably is a burned out fuse. Correct the problem by installing a new fuse in the box under the dash.

Still another problem with the heater, common at the start of the winter driving season, is recurring air bubbles in the heater hose. The one symptom is a barely noticeable flow of heat from the heater even after the engine has been running for some time with the heater and fan on. (See illustration on next page.)

To rid the system of air bubbles, slide the heater knob on your dashboard to "hot" and turn on the engine. Then get outside, raise the hood and find the heater inlet and return hoses on the engine wall. Touch both hoses until you have determined which is warmer and which is colder. Remove the clamp from the cold hose near the engine wall and slide it out of the way, then twist the hose until it turns and wiggle it free of its mounting.

Now hold the hose in your hands for a few moments to permit the coolant to drain and the air bubbles to disperse. Then put the hose back the way you found it and check the heat flow inside the car. If there is no improvement, keep wiggling the hose until the heat picks up. When the flow of warm air is satisfactory, the bubbles are gone, so replace the heater hose clamp and shut the hood.

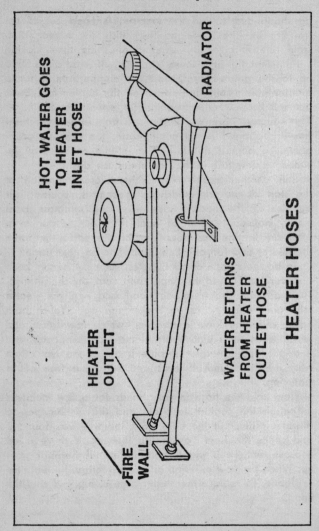

HOT WATER GOES TO HEATER INLET HOSE

RADIATOR

WATER RETURNS FROM HEATER OUTLET HOSE

HEATER OUTLET

FIRE WALL

HEATER HOSES

Lights, Accessories, Action

Anyone with enough mechanical ability to replace a light bulb in his favorite reading lamp should have no trouble installing new lights in his car. The only problem a motorist may have is in knowing when certain lights have burned out. Auto manufacturers have been considerate enough to provide clues right on the dashboard.

The directional flashers on the dash are the key to trouble. When one of them stops blinking, or quits making that clicking noise when it does blink, it does not necessarily mean that it is out of order. In fact, such is unlikely.

Get outside and check your directional signal lights at the front and back of the car. Probably one of them has burned out. If so, unscrew the lens, push the bulb slightly inward, give it a quarter turn to the left and remove it. Replace it and the dashboard light should resume working.

It is only when you signal for a turn and no lights flash on the dashboard that the bulb is out on the dashboard flasher. If both flasher lights go on, but do not blink, the problem lies with the flasher unit. Easily accessible under the dash near the steering column, it plugs directly into the fuse box. You should have no trouble at all in plugging in a new one. (See illustration on next page.)

If a cluster of lights on your dash goes out, the problem may be with a fuse. Check the fuse box for any fuse with a burned out metal strip inside the glass tube. Replace it with a fuse of the same size, by snapping out the old one with a screwdriver and pushing in the new one with your finger. Fuses which burn out time and again are pointing to trouble in the electrical system, so see a mechanic.

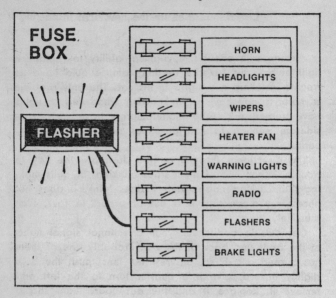

To replace a headlight, check the trim around the light for Phillips-head screws and unscrew them. Remove the trim, if necessary, and then find the three slotted screws which secure the metal rim around the headlight. Remove them with a regular screwdriver, take off the rim and tilt the headlight outward. Behind it you will find a plastic plug from which three wires lead to the lamp. Disconnect these wires.

Examine the metal prongs for signs of corrosion. Even if it seems that the light has burned out, it may be that the prongs have rusted and all that is needed to reclaim them is a little sanding. You might save yourself the cost of a new headlight by reconnecting the plug on the old one and testing it.

If your original diagnosis was correct, get rid of the

burned out lamp and pick up the new one, inspecting it for markings that indicate which end is up. On most lamps these are in the form of the word "Top" or an arrow. If you find neither, just make sure that the embossed letters on the glass are right side up.

Holding the new lamp in position, reconnect the plastic plug to the prongs and have someone turn on the headlights, or, if necessary, do so yourself. If the lamp goes on, slide it into the headlight housing, replace the metal rim and the three slotted screws and put back the metal trim, securing it with the Phillips-head screws.

Every now and then, when there's nary a Hospital Zone sign to be seen, hit your horn just to see that it still is working. If the pedestrians on the street turn toward you, the horn is fine. But, if they jump into the air, it is too loud. If they do nothing at all—even though you heard something—the horn is too low. Thank the pedestrians for their help and later, in a nice quiet spot, get out your pliers, screwdriver and wrench and adjust the volume of the horn.

On most cars, the horn is located directly behind the grill and, once you've found it, use the pliers to bend the tabs on the bottom of the cover and gently peel it away. Take a good look at the actuating mechanism. In the center, you will find a small screw and a stud nut. The screw is the horn's volume control and turning it clockwise should make the horn sound softer, while counterclockwise should have the opposite effect. If you are fixing the horn with the help of an assistant whose job it is to sound the horn after you have adjusted the screw, stuff a rag into the horn to keep from being deafened. When you are satisfied with the volume, lock the nut and replace the cover. Don't forget to remove the rag from the horn.

If ever your horn sticks on you, do not take apart the mechanism to try and learn the cause. Just pull out the wires. The neighbors will be grateful. Later, when things have quieted down, drive your car to a mechanic.

Don't mess around with your car radio. Probably it is transistorized and should be serviced only by a pro. However, you can save a good deal of the cost of having your radio repaired if you remove it from the car yourself.

Begin by tugging the control knobs off the front of the radio and then removing the retaining nut from each stem with a wrench. Disconnect the speaker, power and ground wires. If they are not color-coded, mark each with a piece of adhesive tape so that you will know where to reconnect them at the proper time. Now unplug the thick antenna cable from the right side of the radio and slide the radio out of the dash.

One car radio problem that does not require the services of a technician is weak reception. By properly adjusting a device known as the antenna trimmer, you may be able to improve your reception without help.

Start by turning on the radio and setting the tuner at 1400 on your AM dial. If there is no station, get used to the static because it is all you are going to hear for the next few minutes. Slither down onto the floor beneath the dash so that you can get a good look at the radio and then locate the antenna wire on the right side. Beside it you should find a small hole or a six-sided knob, often marked with the word "trim." With your fingers or a small screwdriver, slowly turn the trimmer until the sound of a station comes into focus. Continue adjusting the trimmer until the station becomes as clear as it can get. So will every other station within reach.

Windshield wipers are no more immune to the weather they are supposed to protect against than the other rubber parts of your car. The wiper blades—the rubber parts that come into contact with the windshield—

should be checked from time to time for signs of cracking and fraying. If they need replacing, be certain that you purchase the proper refill blade for your car.

Generally, these can be divided into two categories according to the method of installation. One is equipped with a plastic button on the metal frame. When the button is pressed, the blade is released from the frame. The lock closes automatically when a new rubber blade is pressed into place. The other blade, known as the bayonet type, comes with a couple of small metal tabs, which, when pinched together, allows the end of the blade to be inserted in the wiper frame. To remove the blade, just bring the tabs together and slide it out. To install a new blade, slide it into the frame and listen for the click that tells you it is secure.

After installing new wiper blades, always make certain that no metal part of the frame is touching the windshield. The alternative may be a neatly inscribed arc in the glass.

If the problem with your windshield wipers is the metal arm (vandals love bending them back from the windshield), purchase the proper replacement from a dealer. Install by pulling the old arm out of the shaft and pushing the new arm down into position.

Another annoying problem, especially in winter when your car is bathed in road salt every few minutes, is a malfunctioning windshield washer. Nine times out of ten, the problem is simply that the reservoir is out of fluid; or, in winter, out of anti-freeze. If the reservoir is full, you'll have to do some further investigating to find out just what the problem is. (See illustration on next page).

Begin by examining the washer hose along its entire length from the reservoir to where it disappears in the firewall. Check for holes, breaks and pinches. If you find nothing, try poking a paper clip into the

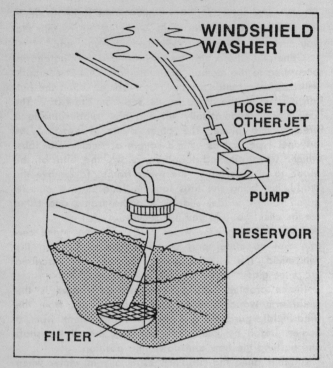

WINDSHIELD WASHER

HOSE TO OTHER JET

PUMP

RESERVOIR

FILTER

water jets directly in front of the windshield in the hood cowl. Often the jets become gummed up with dirt and ice and, if you can chip the stuff away, the problem may be solved.

Another place to look for trouble is in the reservoir itself. To prevent dirt from being sucked into the washer system, there's a small piece of screen at the bottom of the reservoir. If it has done its job so well that the opening now is choked with crud, remove the reservoir and empty it of fluid and dirt. Then install new fluid. If the piece of screen is attached to the end of the hose in the cap, just snap off the cap and wipe it clean. As a last resort, check the washer system fuse in the fuse box. It may be the cause of your problems.

The most hazardous part of the car for the amateur auto repair person might well be the air conditioning system. (See illustration below.) This is because the refrigerant, Freon, can cause painful frostbite if it touches your skin, blindness if it gets in your eyes and gives off toxic fumes when it burns. If you haven't already lost your nerve, there still is one relatively safe procedure that anyone can perform on an auto air con-

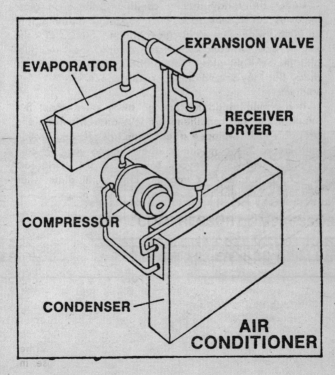

ditioning system without risking life or limb. And that is a check of the refrigerant level.

Sit in the front seat and turn on the engine and air conditioner. If you just aren't satised with the temperature of the air coming through the vents, wait a few minutes for the air conditioner to achieve maximum efficiency. If it still is giving off only minimally cooled or warm air, get outside, raise the hood and begin hunting for the "sight glass." You should find it on a component called the receiver-dryer—a long, cylindrical device usually connected to the air conditioner condenser.

Under every day driving conditions, the sight glass becomes caked with road dirt. So, using a damp rag, carefully wipe the sight glass clean. Then, with the engine and air conditioner still running, look for bubbles in the sight glass. You probably will see many of them, but they should begin to disappear within a few moments.

If the bubbles do not just go away after about five minutes, the air conditioner is low on refrigerant and probably has developed a leak. Don't risk fooling around with Freon. See a mechanic about having your air conditioner recharged. If your car passed the refrigerant level test, but bubbles appear in the sight glass when you turn off the engine, don't worry. That is normal.

Body Workout

Now that we've got things pretty well straightened out under the hood, it's time we paid some attention to the hood itself, or to any other part of the exterior that's beginning to show its age. Despite the various claims of auto manufacturers, wax and polish companies and painters, you can be sure that some traces of rust will pierce your car's defenses.

Body rot is as certain as death and taxes and much more insidious because, once it makes the barest headway, it will spread until either you stop it, or your car begins to look like a piece of Swiss cheese. Long before the holes appear, you should tackle any signs of rust head-on. To do this properly, you will need the use of an electric drill, sandpaper and sanding disc.

With a No. 50 grit sandpaper disc, sand down the rust spot until all signs of corrosion are gone and only the bare metal is visible. If an indentation is left, mix some body filler by carefully following the directions printed on the package and apply it accordingly. Sand down any excess and let dry.

Use a piece of No. 80 grit sandpaper to hand sand the filler until it is perfectly smooth to the touch and flush with the metal. Correct any remaining grooves by smearing a thin layer of spot putty with a plastic spreader and let dry. Resume hand sanding the area with No. 80 paper. When you are done, dampen a rag with solvent and clean the area.

If, by the time you are ready to counter-attack, that rust spot already has gone all the way through the metal, don't despair. Act quickly and you still have time to kill this cancer before it devastates your car. In addition to the electric sander, you will need a body repair kit whose essentials must include a plastic scraper, fiberglass cloth, body filler and hardener.

Begin by using a No. 50 grit sandpaper disc to scrape the corrosion down to the bare metal. Keep sanding until you have scraped a ring of bare metal about three inches wide, all around the hole. This should guarantee that all the rust is gone. If it is not, it soon will begin spreading again, eating away at both the sheet metal and the repair.

Force the metal surrounding the hole inward at a 45 degree angle by beating it with a ball-peen hammer. Then cut a piece of the fiberglass cloth slightly bigger than the hole. Before placing it over the hole, mix some body filler and hardener and apply a thick coating to the beaten metal.

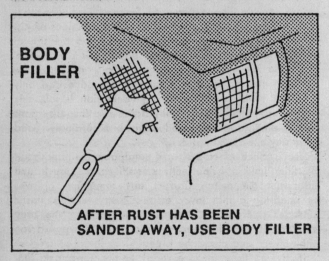

BODY FILLER

AFTER RUST HAS BEEN
SANDED AWAY, USE BODY FILLER

Now place the fiberglass cloth over the hole, pushing the edges into the soft filler material. When it is secure, smooth the filler flat against the metal with the plastic scraper. (See illustration.)

Wait for the filler to harden and then mix another

batch sufficient to cover the entire piece of fiberglass cloth. Use the spreader to apply the compound evenly over the cloth. Trim away the excess with a knife before it hardens.

Once the second application of compound hardens, smooth it with a No. 50 grit sanding disc and then mix up a third batch of filler compound to apply to any imperfections which might still be present. The third application of compound should be smoothed with No. 80 grit sandpaper after it hardens.

Spot putty should be applied to any shallow grooves remaining. After it has dried, hand sand with No. 80 grit sandpaper and clean it with solvent. The repair is ready for priming and painting.

Now that you've done a job on that cavity a dentist might be proud of, don't ruin it by neglecting to apply primer before you paint. The primer serves a dual purpose, evening minor rough spots on the surface to be painted and helping to hold the paint to the metal.

Before applying the primer and paint, it is necessary to border the repair with newspaper and masking tape to prevent spattering on adjacent areas. The job is just as easy as it sounds, if you follow one rule. Always use masking tape. It has been designed especially for jobs such as these and peels off without leaving any telltale marks, as other tapes will.

Run a strip of masking tape along the edge of a newspaper page so that about half the width of the tape is on the paper. Then press the exposed edge of the tape against a side of the area that's going to be painted so the surrounding metal is covered by the newspaper. Repeat the process until the entire area is bordered. In general, make sure you have protected the surface up to three feet away from the area you are going to paint (see illustration). Take special care in taping chrome, metal trim and glass. The tiniest piece of tape extending from these irregularly shaped surfaces onto the metal to be painted will leave an annoying line.

PAINT MASKING

MASK AREA TO BE PAINTED WITH NEWSPAPERS AND MASKING TAPE

If this is the first time you've ever applied primer to a car, it might be a good idea to take some target practice with your spray can. A suitable target is a piece of newspaper taped to a garage wall, or, better yet, a tin can. Hold the spray can about a foot away from the target and try to cover it with a fine spray of primer. This will be easiest if you move the spray can from side to side in a smooth, non-arcing stroke. Target practice should help you develop a light touch with the spray.

Now that you've got the hang of it, apply the primer to your car in the same easy manner. Ideally, you want to cover the afflicted area with a number of light coats, rather than one heavy one which probably will run. It will take about five minutes for each coat of primer to dry, so give yourself enough time to finish the job since you probably will need two or three coats.

Give the primer about a quarter of an hour to dry and then apply a light coat of auto body glazing putty. Give the putty an hour to dry and then lightly sand with a wet piece of 320 wet-or-dry sandpaper on a sanding block. Apply a final coat of primer.

At last, it is time to apply the paint. Check the vehicle identification plate on the firewall, or the owner's manual, for the code number of the proper color. Your auto supply dealer will cross reference the number in his catalogue to give you the exact color paint you need.

If you've never painted a car before, it is time for some more target practice. When you feel comfortable with the spray can, shake it one more time to make sure the paint is mixed well and then apply it to the car with the same even, non-arcing stroke you used with the primer. Once again, do not try to finish the job with a single heavy coat of paint. Use two or three fine coats for more pleasing results. Remember to keep your hand moving. If you hold the can in one spot, the paint will run. The same thing will happen if you move the can too slowly.

Allow four or five days for the job to dry properly and then dampen a rag with rubbing compound and work it gently into the paint. The rubbing compound is a very gentle abrasive and its use helps the new paint blend with the old. If the match isn't perfect, don't fret. After a few weeks of exposure to the elements and normal road dirt, the new paint will be almost impossible to spot.

Now that you've restored your car's finish to its pristine elegance, let's see what you can do about keeping it that way. For starters, make it a point to periodically hose down the underbody. That flushes away harmful road salts and also eliminates build-ups of mud and grime in such inaccessible places as fender wells and the inside of bumpers. While you're at it, train the hose on the transmission case, the underside of the engine block, the driveshaft, rear axle and exhaust system.

In time, rust spots probably will appear on your bumpers anyway, the inevitable result of dents and nicks which pierce the metal plating. To get rid of them, rub them with steelwool and then apply some naval jelly. After waiting the time specified on the container, wash the jelly off with water and wipe dry. Then shine the area with paste wax.

Because dirt is the number one enemy of a bright finish, wash your car often, flushing away the dirt before it can eat into the metal and cause rust. Never wash your car in the sun, or when the hood is still warm from a drive. The heat will cause streaking. Don't waste your time trying to wash away tough spots such as tree sap, bird droppings or road tar without softening them first. Use a commercially prepared solvent—not elbow grease. Hard rubbing may result in damage to the paint job. If you're in a hurry and don't have any solvent at hand, raid the kitchen cupboard for corn oil. It's slower than the professional stuff, but just about as effective.

The best protection for a car's finish is a high quality, hard automotive paste wax that leaves a protective coating over the paint. Never apply it without first washing and polishing your car. Polish, you may be surprised to find, is not the same as wax. It is a slightly abrasive substance which helps bring out the hidden beauty of a stale paint job by scraping away layers of old wax and oxidized paint. Always follow the directions on the can of paste wax and polish scrupulously. Clean your car's vinyl roof only with products designed especially for that job.

Just because it is not open to public scrutiny is no reason for you to neglect your car's interior. Rugs should be vacuumed regularly and rubber floor mats and vinyl or leather upholstery should be cleaned just as often. To do that best, after dusting rub some rubber lubricant, or neutral soap or very gentle detergent onto a clean sponge and massage it into the material until it foams. Be careful not to use too much. Then, with a damp towel, wipe the lather away. After the entire area has dried, wipe it again with a clean cotton cloth. Always attack stains as soon as they occur. If this is impractical, a commercial upholstery stain remover is for you.

As long as we're on the topic of cleanliness, let's not forget about your car's engine. From time to time you should remove the caked grease and dirt that inevitably collects there. To do this you will need spray cans of water soluble degreaser and moisture disperser. Water, plenty of rags and a scraper also will come in handy.

Warm up the engine and, after turning off the ignition, raise the hood and use the scraper to remove the thickest deposits of filth. Then spray all areas to be cleaned with the degreaser and give the stuff some time to soak in. Use a garden hose to flush away the dirt, making sure to keep the water away from the carburetor and distributor.

If the engine remains dirty, repeat the procedure as many times as necessary. After the water has run off, spray the ignition wires with the moisture dispersing fluid to insure a quick start. Then shut the hood and turn on the ignition. The heat generated by the engine will evaporate any moisture.

Healthy, Wealthy and Wise
Behind The Wheel

You're moving down the highway at 50 miles per hour, when, up ahead, you see the green light turning amber. Automatically your right foot moves from the accelerator to the brake pedal—and plunges straight to the floorboards. What to do?

Well, for a start, don't panic. Try pumping the brake pedal a few times. Sometimes your brakes will come back as suddenly as they vanished. If nothing happens, try your parking brake. Don't hit it too hard, especially on a curve. All you'll succeed in doing that way is to throw the car into a spin. Apply the pressure gently and then shift into a lower gear.

If all else fails and you are about to plow into another car or a stationary object, try sideswiping something like a highway guardrail or even a parked car or two. Remember, a sideswipe is an indirect hit and always preferable to a head-on collision. If you must resort to a sideswipe to halt your car, make sure your liability insurance is paid up. If you prefer to crash head-on, make sure you've paid your hospitalization insurance.

Undaunted by that unfortunate experience with your brakes, you're barreling down the highway again when your left front tire blows and your car suddenly lurches into incoming traffic. Again, panic is your greatest enemy. Don't lose your head and slam down on the brakes or tug hard at the steering wheel. You probably will lose complete control of the car that way. Instead, stop giving the car gas and hang on to the steering wheel, gently trying to steer back to your side of the road as your car slows down. When you have regained control, pull off the road onto the right shoulder. Now it is safe to slowly apply your brake.

Should the blowout occur on a rear tire, your car will not react as violently. However, you should handle the emergency as you would a front-tire blowout.

If you survive a high-speed blowout, then a high-speed skid shouldn't present any problem at all. Once more, it is imperative that you do not lose your head and slam on the brakes. To get out of trouble you will have to steer out of the skid, something that is impossible if the brakes are locked.

Once you feel your car moving sideways, get off the gas and turn the steering wheel into the direction of the skid. As your car straightens out, you will regain control quickly. You must resist the natural urge to steer away from the skid. That will not bring the car back into the proper direction and will cause you to lose even more control.

It is not always your own car that is the greatest danger to life and limb. One of the most unpleasant highway experiences you can have is to see an oncoming car headed straight at you in your lane. No matter how tempting it may be to swerve to the left and pass him on the wrong side, don't do it. There is a very good chance that the other driver may realize his error and veer into the proper lane—the one you just entered. Always, **always**, swerve to the right to avoid a collision. Even if it means sideswiping another car, or a guardrail, or banging hard into a curb, remember that anything is better than a head-on crash.

The most terrifying experience for any motorist is to find himself and his car sinking in deep water. Incredible as it may seem, this rotten luck strikes almost 4000 drivers in this country every year. The survivors were among those who acted quickest.

Don't wait for your car to stop sinking before making your escape. In fact, if you're lucky, the car may float for a few seconds, precious time to get away. Immediately unfasten your safety belt, roll down the window and climb out. Acting fast is especially important if your car is equipped with power windows, which may short out if the operating mechanism becomes wet.

If you find it impossible to get out the window, try the door. Don't panic if it will not open right away. The pressure of the water pushing against the outside of the door is too much to fight. Just wait a few seconds. As water enters the passenger compartment, the pressure will begin to equalize and you will be able to open the door. If the totally unthinkable happens and your car lands on its left side while you're still trapped behind the wheel, utilize the air pocket which will form on the passenger side above you. This air may give you time to open the window, or door and escape.

Two less dangerous, but equally frightening mishaps are stuck accelerators or hoods that fly up while you are driving at top speed.

If your gas pedal becomes stuck to the car floorboards while you are on the highway, use the tip of your shoe to nudge it up. That failing, put the car into neutral and slow down with the brake. There are two nonos in this situation. Never reach down with your hand to free the stuck pedal. That will cause you to take your eyes off the road longer than is safe. If there is a passenger in the front seat with you, it is his job. And never, never switch off the ignition. That was common procedure years ago when cars did not come equipped with automatic steering column locks. Today, all you might accomplish by twisting the key is to lose complete control of your car.

If your vision is obscured by a flying hood covering the windshield, avoid slamming on the brakes. Try peering through the narrow space between the bottom of the hood and the dashboard while gently applying the brakes. Your next best choice is to stick your head out the window for a look at the road as you gradually slow the car. It might be a good idea to find out which way works better for you before you have to employ one or the other in an emergency.

When the weather turns to rain, the smart driver cuts his speed and drops back a couple of additional car lengths behind the vehicles in front of him. Unless it is absolutely necessary, don't slam the brakes, floor the accelerator or tug hard at the wheel on a wet road. The result probably will be a skid at best, hydroplaning at worst.

Drive very slowly through deep puddles to keep water out of the ignition system and pump your brakes a couple of times when you're back on dry land—just to see if you have them before you need them. If you don't, downshift to a lower gear and touch the brake pedal lightly. Driving a short distance should dry them out.

In foggy weather, when your vision is obscured, don't use your high beams. The bright lights reflect off the moisture in the air and what you see is mostly glare. Use your low beams, which are aimed closer to the road in front of the car. Fog lights are best of all. If you don't have a set, think about buying them. They aren't expensive and if they save your life just once are quite a bargain.

If the weather gets so bad that you feel you must get off the road, pull over to the right shoulder as far as you can go and turn on your flashers. It is a good idea to carry flares in your emergency kit and if you have one now is a good time to use it. Light it and place it about 150 feet behind your car. If you have neither flasher, nor flares, do not leave your tail lights on. An approaching motorist might mistakenly think you are on the road and moving and plough into the rear of your car before he realizes his error.

The safest driver is the defensive driver, who always expects the worst of the other motorist and is prepared for it if it should come. In bad weather, a defensive driver also takes into consideration the road. Thousands of road signs proclaim that in cold weather a particular bridge will freeze before the surface of the road. But the signs don't tell you what to do about it. The answer is simple—drive defensively. Hit your brake and slow your car before you reach the bridge. The last thing you need is to go into an icy skid on a narrow bridge. If the ice appears so suddenly that there is no time to hit the brake before you are upon it, take your foot off the accelerator and try to glide through it, avoiding, if you can, tugging at the wheel.

The rudest motorist is the night driver who fails to dim his brights for oncoming traffic. Much as you may feel the desire for revenge, restrain yourself from emulating his pigish behavior. Never flash your own high beams into his eyes. Two blind drivers coming head on are infinitely more dangerous than just one. Trust the rude one not to slam into you (you can be sure he doesn't want to) and avert your eyes from his headlights by glancing at the yellow line or shoulder at the right side of the road.

Night driving also is tired driving. If you feel fatigue coming on, don't attempt to fight it. You may not succeed all the time. Instead, pull off the road at the first wide spot on the shoulder, or at a rest area, and *shut off the engine*. Roll up the windows, leaving an inch or two for fresh air and lock the doors to keep out intruders. Sweet dreams! You will find the half an hour or so that you lose napping will more than be made up for in safety and driving comfort.

If ever you have to get out of a disabled car, always

stand behind it, rather than in front. Because careless motorists strike vehicles on the road shoulder with alarming frequency, you could be struck and injured, or worse, by your own rolling car. It is always safest to stand behind the vehicle to flag down a tow truck and wave off approaching traffic. You can see someone heading directly for you, too, and react.

Another of motoring's rare, but supremely discomforting crises, is getting stuck in snow. Serious snow. The kind that buries roads and sometimes cars and leaves you no choice but to wait for rescue by snowplow, or helicopter or dogsled. Unless you were resourceful enough to have brought your cross-country skis with you, it is best to stay with the car, no matter how deep the snow gets. You'd be surprised at what an excellent shelter your vehicle is against the elements.

In the grim winter of 1976-1977, highway rescue crews in Ohio found a truck driver frost-bitten, but otherwise safe, in the cab of his truck after being lost and presumed dead for more than a week following a blizzard. Although his truck had been buried by the high snows and he had had nothing to eat, there was plenty of melted snow to drink and enough air reached him to keep him alive.

Presumably, you won't have to spend a week in your car before being rescued. But, if you find yourself in serious trouble in deep snow, act as if you're going to be there a while. Don't run your engine and heater continually. You will be surprised at how fast that will deplete your fuel. Keep them on for only ten minutes every hour. Your car will retain enough warmth to keep you reasonably comfortable and you will maintain a reliable supply of fuel.

Even though it means that you will be a little bit colder than you would prefer, always keep a window open an inch or two to allow fresh air in the passengers' compartment. Equally important, get outside and make sure the snow isn't covering your tailpipe. If it is, you must dig it away. A blocked tailpipe will cause poisonous auto exhausts, such as carbon monoxide, to back up inside. The CO is colorless, odorless and makes you drowsy. If you are overcome by it, you may not get a second chance.

While you are outside the car, digging out the tailpipe—which should be checked at least once every 45 minutes in a heavy snowfall—tie a brightly colored scarf, or other piece of cloth, to the radio antenna to signal rescuers. Now also is a good time to light one of the flares you have been saving for a real emergency.

If there are passengers in the back seat, turn on the dome light from time to time to check on their condition. It is generally colder in the back seat and less well-ventilated than the front.

Gasoline is dangerous stuff, so don't treat it lightly. Don't use it to clean your car, or as a solvent. It vaporizes very easily and gas vapor is explosive. Don't even carry a reserve supply of gasoline in your trunk, unless it is contained in a sturdy, gasoline safety can with a spring cap and a flame arrester in the neck. Because gasoline is such a volatile substance, it always is a good idea to keep a small chemical fire extinguisher in your car. But, if your car catches fire and it looks like it is getting out of control, throw away the extinguisher and start running. If the flames reach the gas tank, the explosion may incinerate everything in the immediate vicinity.

Whenever possible, keep your gas tank full. The less air in the tank, the slower the evaporation of its expensive contents. It is also a good idea to avoid letting your gas gauge go all the way down. When your car is running on a nearly empty tank, rust and dirt which normally lay on the bottom are sucked into the fuel system and can gum up the works.

No matter what you may have heard to the contrary, there is no reason for you ever to put high test gas in an auto engine requiring regular. Gas mileage will not increase and the cost of premium is, of course, much greater than regular.

It is absolutely imperative, however, that you do not put regular gas in a high compression engine which requires premium. Rather than save you money on gasoline costs, it will lead to lousy performance and extremely high repair bills.

If a car thief wants your car—and somewhere there's probably one who does—don't let him have it without putting up a fight. Always lock the doors, roll the windows tight and never keep a spare set of keys anywhere in your car. Never leave your car with the engine running. **And make sure you haven't left your keys in the ignition.**

Whenever you park in a driveway, or in an untended lot, keep the front of your car toward the street. If anyone tries to "hot-wire" the ignition—the most common way for a thief to start a car without the key—he will run a greater risk of being spotted by someone passing along the sidewalk. If you must leave your car overnight, select a well-lighted area. That discourages both car thieves and car strippers, who can reduce a fully loaded cream puff to a hollow shell in less than 20 minutes.

If the strippers do attack your car, you can probably kiss the stolen parts good-bye. Most professional car thieves will use acid to etch away the identifying serial numbers. But it doesn't hurt to try marking some of the valuable parts in two places—one obvious and the other where the thieves might not be so quick to look. Another idea is to drop a slip of paper with your name and address into one car window slot. Remember, however, that one piece of paper with your name and address on it which you never should leave in your car is your registration—unless the law in your state requires it.

The only way to guarantee that you never will have any valuables stolen from your car is not to leave them inside when you park. In most big cities, thefts from cars have reached epidemic proportions. One enterprising New Yorker turned this sorry situation to his advantage during a garbage strike a few years back. Each morning, he gift-wrapped his garbage in paper from a Fifth Avenue department store and tied it with a bow. Then he placed it in full view on the front seat of his convertible, which he always parked with the top down (thereby also foiling the random vandal who delights in slashing them). When he came back to the car, the package and its offending contents were, without fail, gone.

IDENTIFICATION NUMBERS

License Plate _____

Registration _____

Serial _____

Engine _____